Treatment Guide of Selected DSM IV & V Diagnoses

First Edition

Farideh Fazlian, PhD

Dog Ear Publishing

© 2013 Farideh Fazlian, PhD
Typeset/Editor: Jeff Cutright

All Rights Reserved.

No part of this publication may be reproduced, stored in a retrieval system, or transmitted, in any form or by any means, electronic, mechanical, photocopying, recording, or otherwise, without the written permission of the author.

Limit of Liability/Disclaimer of Warrantee: While the author and publisher have made their best efforts in preparing this publication, they make no warrantees with respect to the completeness of the contents of this book. The particular approaches and strategies presented herein may not be suitable for every condition. You may consult with an experienced professional in the field where appropriate. This book is designed to offer useful clinical information in regard to the subject of treatment planning. In this regard neither the author nor the publisher shall be liable for any damages.

This edition published by
Dog Ear Publishing
4010 W. 86th Street, Ste H
Indianapolis, IN 46268

www.dogearpublishing.net

ISBN: 978-1-4575-2287-1
This book is printed on acid-free paper.

Printed in the United States of America

To my mother
and
To memory of my beloved father

Contents

Preface   vii
Introduction   ix

Part I.
Treatment Planning and Intervention: The Selected Mental Health Disorders in Children and Adolescents   1

  -Attention Deficit Hyperactivity Disorder   5

  -Conduct Disorder   9

  -Oppositional Defiant Disorder   13

Part II.
Treatment Planning and Intervention: The Selected Mental Health Disorder of Adults   17

  -Adjustment Disorder   21

  -Anxiety Disorder   25

  -Bipolar Disorders   29

  -Depressive Disorder   33

  -Eating Disorder   39

  -Mood Disorder Due to G.M.C.   43

  -Posttraumatic Stress Disorder   49

  -Substance Use Disorder   55

  -Schizophrenic Disorders   61

Part III.
Treatment Planning and Intervention: The Personality Disorders of Adults   67

  -Antisocial Personality Disorder   71

  -Avoidant Personality Disorder   75

Contents

-Borderline Personality Disorder — 79

-Dependent Personality Disorder — 83

-Histrionic Personality Disorder — 87

-Schizoid Personality Disorder — 91

References — 95

Preface

Compiling this book has taken several years after the first I conceptualized it as a resource and guideline for development of effective treatment plans for many mental/emotional illnesses. While I was putting part of my work together, I have come to the conclusion that developing a comprehensive treatment intervention plan has been a sensitive and significant part of the treatment process and positive outcome of the treatment by clinicians in the domain of therapy. Furthermore in this regard, treatment becomes more effective if a clinician considers working with the patients/clients through the stages of the severity and intensity of their emotional/mental suffering. In the development of this resource and guideline book, both "stages "and "intensity" factors were addressed as significant in the development of a treatment plan.

Initial conceptualization of a basic Treatment Plan Guideline resulted from a successful experience for me in the presentation of an Oral Licensing Exam years ago. As my world of clinical practice as a licensed psychologist required increased responsibility at an extended and demanding level, I have found it very helpful to apply my basic treatment planning guideline while simultaneously making changes and improving the effectiveness of that plan. Most of the changes and improvements of the effectiveness of "Treatment Plans" have resulted from the application of different methods and strategies of identified treatment issues related to emotional/mental condition.

Throughout years of practice as a clinician I have found it very enlightening and helpful to listen to other clinicians concerning the effectiveness or lack of effectiveness of my approach in treatment. I received additional input from my clients regarding the effectiveness of an applied method and strategy on the change, improvement, and recovery of an identified treatment issue/problem. Furthermore, the outcome of the ongoing application of a Treatment Plan Guideline over the years has helped me on improving the effectiveness of the plans presented in this resource and guide book. However, I definitely believe that there is opportunity for further improvement for this Treatment Plan Guideline in the future as it will be applied and practiced by other clinicians.

Preface

It is my earnest hope that this resource guideline book will be helpful for those clinicians interested in developing comprehensive treatment plans for their patients/clients in their clinical work.

Introduction

This book is intended to serve as a resource and guideline for developing treatment plans and formulating useful and practical clinical methods and strategies for dealing with psychological disorders, conditions and symptoms. The core purpose of writing this resource and guideline book has been: 1) to share a structured guide or framework with clinicians and to a certain extent with interns about development of a treatment plan while taking into account the intensity, immediacy, and stages of the identified mental health conditions. 2) to provide a guide for identifying treatment issues related to a specific mental disorder and establishing treatment goals for a mental health condition or identified problem/issue. 3) to provide a guideline for practitioners in selecting methods of intervention and development of effective strategies addressing specific identified issues related to a particular mental health disorder, and 4) to offer a resource book for young clinicians or interns who face challenges in the application of academic knowledge to the clinical domain.

In the process of compiling this book, which is part of the outcome of my own clinical experience over the years, I have seen significant changes in the area of patient/client treatment. Although all of the changes that have been brought about by many authors at various levels overall have helped the effectiveness of treatment planning, I believe that patient/client participation in treatment planning has been one of the most significant changes in this domain. Therefore, the application of the treatment planning suggested in this resource and guideline book is considered to be the most effective when it takes into consideration patient/client participation in the development of a treatment plan.

In the development of a treatment plan using this guide book, the most severe identified problem is considered to be addressed initially and immediately. However, some of the residual problems related to the initial stage of intervention may extend into the next stage of the treatment, or to the short-term intervention stage as it may be feasible. The methods and strategies that are used to address symptoms and problems related to an identified mental or emotional condition at a selected stage of intervention may require reasonable modifications if they are feasible and necessary for an effective

Introduction

intervention purpose. Structured types of intervention approaches may be considered effective for a desirable therapeutic outcome when a patient/client is considered to have responded well to the intervention addresses a crisis and the initial stage of intense emotional/mental suffering.

Directive, supportive and problem solving methods of intervention are considered to be the most effective in reduction of intense emotional pain and suffering caused by mental/emotional disturbances. As the patient/client indicates preparedness for further changes and improvements, then intervention at the intermediate stage of therapy for mental/emotional suffering is to be addressed with the application of some of the suggested methods and strategies of the "short-term treatment plan," prior to advancing to the long-term stage of treatment.

In this resource and guideline book potential identified weaknesses, treatment issues, and problems relevant to the mental disorder are listed. In the application of the suggested methods and strategies to develop a treatment plan, clinicians should consider not only the patient's/client's identified problems, symptoms and weaknesses, but also the patient's/client's strengths. In the application of the methods and strategies suggested in this book for writing an effective Treatment Plan, clinicians may proceed by using a structured interview of the patient/client, and if it is applicable, interviewing a family member, significant other, or a staff member who works with or knows the patient. Often after a structured interview, the clinician should use a less structured interview, where the patient/client feels more comfortable in disclosing additional personal information is very valuable in collecting data on the patient's/client's assets, strengths and needs for the formulation of an effective Treatment Plan.

For the purposes of applying the methods and strategies described in this book, the selection and application of appropriate strengths and assets when dealing with an identified symptom, problem or issue must be taken into consideration. However, this exhortation should not be taken to undermine the embodied medical models designed to identify and fix a patient's weakness. Nonetheless, it is crucial to avoid any complications resulting from the patient's demoralization. Thus, the clinician should protect the patient/client by encouraging active participation in the process of developing a treatment plan and including and applying the patient's strengths and assets in the formulation of the plan of intervention.

PART I

Application of Treatment Planning and Intervention: The Selected Mental Disorders in Children and Adolescents

Part I. Application of Treatment Planning and Intervention: The Selected Mental Disorders in Children and Adolescents

Part I is on the treatment planning and intervention of the three selected major mental/behavior diagnoses among children and adolescents. In this section, for each of the selected mental disorders, illustrated treatment plans and interventions are provided for the three stages of the course of the mental health conditions.

The immediate plan of intervention emphasizes treatment goals for maintaining patients' safety, preventing risk and danger to self and others, initiating recovery from acute symptoms, and containing crises contributing to the acute phase of the mental health condition of a child or adolescent. Directive, supportive, and problem-solving methods of intervention are considered to be relevant and effective at this acute stage. Always, risk assessment, determination of the potential danger to self or others, and immediate intervention are critical at this initial stage of intervention. Appropriate intervention at this initial stage is to contain the acute active symptoms and to prepare the child or adolescent for the second stage of the treatment.

In the second stage of treatment, the focus is on active symptoms affecting the child's or adolescent's mental health condition and his/her functioning level. In this stage of treatment, application of therapeutic methods and approaches requires active participation from the affected child or adolescent as well his or her involved parent or guardian. Application of age appropriate cognitive-behavioral therapy and psycho-educational intervention are critical at this stage of the treatment.

The last stage of the treatment focuses on the long-term treatment issues, including longstanding personal attributes such as self-esteem, self-control, and the child or adolescent's relationship with family and others such as teachers. Family therapy and extensive use of psycho-educational intervention approaches are considered to be very

The Selected Mental Disorders in Children and Adolescents

effective and critical at this stage to help the child or adolescent restore shortcomings on the identified treatment issues.

Attention Deficit Hyperactivity Disorder

Immediate Treatment Plan

I. Immediate Concern Treatment Issues
- ◊ Danger to Self
- ◊ Suicide Risk
- ◊ Danger to Others
- ◊ Medical/Physical Problems
- ◊ Substance Abuse
- ◊ Child Abuse
- ◊ Other Crisis

II. Treatment Plan/Goals
- ◊ To assess the severity of immediate concern issues and make appropriate intervention to contain the most severe and potentially dangerous condition.
- ◊ To proceed with the appropriate intervention to contain present and other immediate concern issues.

III. Intervention Methods
- ◊ Directive/Supportive/ Problem Solving Approaches

IV. Strategies

> *** Obtain signed informed consent from the parents or legal guardian (clarify the limits confidentiality in advance and include a clear financial/fee contract.)
> 1. To assess suicide-risk and danger to self and make appropriate intervention to secure safety of the child.
> 2. To assess the danger to others and make appropriate intervention.
> 3. Refer for medical evaluation and medication intervention.
> 4. If child abuse is suspected, proceed to file the necessary mandated report and protect the child's safety.
> 5. Attend to the immediate concern issues related to substance abuse problems and make appropriate intervention (consider the age of the client).

The Selected Mental Disorders in Children and Adolescents

> 6. Clarify if symptoms and presented conditions are not due to a medical condition.
> 7. Attend to the most severe presented crisis and contain it.
> 8. Attend to other immediate concern issues and make appropriate intervention.

Short-Term Treatment Plan

I. Treatment Issues
- Hyperactivity
- Destructive behavior
- Disruptive behavior
- Sleep Problems
- Depressed or unstable mood
- Academic and school problems
- Attention deficit
- Poor concentration
- Impulsivity
- Interpersonal problems
- Eating problems

II. Treatment Plan/Goals
- To decrease and contain symptomatic behavior and conditions.
- To improve coping skills/social skills.
- To deal with academic problems.
- To deal with interpersonal problems related to severe deficit caused by ADHD.

III. Intervention Methods
- Supportive/Cognitive-Behavioral/psycho-educational Approach

IV. Strategies
> 1. Establish therapeutic alliance with the child and working alliance with the child's family.
> 2. Coordinate with a medical doctor to follow up treatment and medication intervention.
> 3. Use <u>Contingency Management Techniques</u> to deal with hyperactivity and unwanted behaviors.

Attention Deficit Hyperactivity Disorder

4. Train/Coordinate with parents and teachers to apply Contingency Management Techniques.
5. Train child about <u>Self-Control</u> and <u>Self-Monitoring</u> Techniques to deal with unwanted behaviors and impulsivity.
6. Train parents and teachers to use Conner Scale to record target behavior measure (measure for change/progress) as treatment continues.
7. Educate both child and parents abut ADHD.
8. Coordinate with school in evaluation and placement of the child in Special Education classes or IEP.
9. Train parents on stimulus control technique and Self-Monitoring Techniques to deal with related sleep problems.
10. Relaxation training for the child to improve coping skills.
11. Deal with the interpersonal and communication problems of the child with parents, teachers, other significant others and peers.

Long-Term Treatment Plan

I. Treatment Issues
- ◊ Poor self-esteem
- ◊ Parent/Child relationship problem
- ◊ Poor self-control
- ◊ Poor relationship problem
- ◊ Poor interpersonal social and academic skills

II. Treatment Plan/Goals
- ◊ To prevent relapse of symptoms.
- ◊ To improve self-control skills.
- ◊ To improve self-esteem.
- ◊ To restructure family and intervene in dynamic contributing to ADHD.
- ◊ To improve interpersonal and social/academic skills.

The Selected Mental Disorders in Children and Adolescents

III. Intervention Methods
- ◊ Family Therapy/Supportive/ Psycho- educational/ Cognitive-Behavioral Approaches

IV. Strategies

1. Educate child client and parents about changes and improvements that prevent from relapse and improve the child's self-control skills.
2. Help child to identify positive changes/accomplishments that improve self-esteem and self-control skills.
3. Deal with issue of peer rejection, expression of feelings and dealing with therapy, and learning to share his/her feelings with parents.
4. To help child with follow-up self-monitoring techniques to maintain progress and improve self-control skills.
5. Use family therapy techniques to deal with family dynamics contributing to ADHD.
6. Use stress management techniques to deal with on-going stress and to improve coping skills.
7. Continue self-monitoring techniques to maintain positive changes, improvements and for prevention from relapse.

Adjunct Treatment (Goals and Strategies)

1. Referral to educational specialist in providing a plan to manage academic-related issues.
2. Positive peer group activities, e.g. experience art groups, activity to improve interpersonal skills.
3. Support group for parents.
4. Referral to speech therapist if needed.
5. Referral to nutritionist to deal with eating and diet-related issues if appropriate.

Conduct Disorder

Immediate Treatment Plan

I. Immediate Concern Treatment Issues
- ◊ Dangerous to Others
- ◊ Suicide Plan/Risk
- ◊ Problems with Law and Legal System
- ◊ Child Abuse
- ◊ Other Crisis

II. Treatment Plan/Goals
- ◊ To assess the severity of immediate concern issues and make appropriate intervention to contain the most severe and potentially dangerous condition.
- ◊ To proceed with the appropriate intervention to contain presented crisis and other immediate concern issues.

III. Intervention Methods
- ◊ Directive/Supportive/ Problem Solving Approaches

IV. Strategies

> *** Obtain signed informed consent from the parents or legal guardian (clarify the limits confidentiality in advance and include a clear financial/fee contract.)
> 1. To assess suicide-risk and danger to self and make appropriate intervention to secure safety of the child.
> 2. To assess the danger to others and make appropriate intervention.
> 3. Refer for medical evaluation and medication intervention.
> 4. If child abuse is suspected, proceed to file the necessary mandated report to C.P.A. and protect the child's safety. (If your client might be abusing other children, proceed the necessary report to C.P.A)
> 5. Make appropriate intervention to deal with immediate issues related to substance abuse.

The Selected Mental Disorders in Children and Adolescents

> 6. Attend to the immediate concern crisis and contain it (court, school or family related issues).
> 7. Attend to any other immediate concern issues and make appropriate intervention.
> 8. Establish rapport and Therapeutic Alliance with the child (be accepting and non-judgmental and offer to help him with court-related problems or other difficult issues). Form an alliance with family (empathize with them).

Short-Term Treatment Plan

I. Treatment Issues
- Problems with Law or Authority
- Antisocial Conduct
- Problems in School (academic/conduct)
- Communication/Interaction problems with family
- Depression
- Agitation/Anger
- Poor coping skills
- Poor social skills

II. Treatment Plan/Goals.
- To decrease and contain symptomatic behavior/conduct.
- To improve coping skills/social skills.
- To deal with court and family related issues.
- To deal with interpersonal problems caused by severe conduct problem.

III. Intervention Methods:
- Supportive/Cognitive-Behavioral/psycho-educational Approaches

IV. Strategies

> 1. Make a treatment plan acceptable to the client, make contract about the treatment goals and kind of incentive for accomplishment of these goals.
> 2. Educate client about his/her conduct and possible <u>consequence</u>.
> 3. Educate parents/legal guardian about conduct disorder of the client and prevention of negative impact of conduct on family.

Conduct Disorder

> 4. Deal with resistance to therapy (educate child about positive outcome and use incentives).
> 5. Use <u>Contingency Management Techniques</u> to deal with conduct and problem behaviors (time out, loss of privilege).
> 6. Train client in using <u>Self-Monitoring Techniques</u> to deal with antisocial conduct, anger and agitation.
> 7. Provide relaxation training to improve coping skills.
> 8. Provide incentive to family to cooperate with treatment (use improvement and positive outcome of the treatment).
> 9. Coordinate with school to deal with academic/conduct problems.
> 10. Use role playing to deal with communication and interaction problems in family.
> 11. Provide reinforcement for positive behavior to maintain progress.

Long-Term Treatment Plan

I. Treatment Issues
- ◊ Parental rejection
- ◊ Boundary issues in family
- ◊ Poor self-esteem
- ◊ Poor interpersonal skills

II. Treatment Plan/ Goals
- ◊ To deal with parental rejection.
- ◊ To deal with boundary issues in family.
- ◊ To improve self-esteem.
- ◊ To prevent relapse of conduct problem.

III. Intervention Methods
- ◊ Supportive/ Cognitive-Behavioral/ Psycho-educational/Family Therapy/ Appropriate Insight Oriented Therapy

The Selected Mental Disorders in Children and Adolescents

IV. Strategies

1. Educate and help client to identify positive changes and improvements to help with self esteem.
2. Restructure family boundaries contributing to child's conduct problem (i.e. inflexible boundaries or inconsistent boundaries).
3. Deal with and educate family's perception of child's problems.
4. Help client to express his/her feelings about parental rejection; educate family about the impact of their interaction and relation on child.
5. Use Role Playing to improve family interaction/communication.
6. Coordinate with parole/court and school to prevent relapse of conduct problem.
7. Continue self-monitoring techniques to maintain positive change, improvement and prevention from relapse.

Adjunct Treatment (Goals and Strategies)

1. Support and self-help group for child (share feelings)
2. Support group for parents.
3. Peer activities group
4. Sport activities
5. Homework for positive family activities (recreation).

Oppositional Defiant Disorder

Immediate Treatment Plan

I. Immediate Concern Treatment Issues
1. Dangerous to Others
2. Suicide Plan/Risk
3. Recent Child Abuse
4. Child Abuse History
5. Other crisis

II. Treatment Plan/Goals
- ◊ To assess the severity of immediate concern issues and make appropriate intervention to contain the most severe and potentially dangerous condition.
- ◊ To proceed with the appropriate intervention to contain presented crisis and other immediate concern issues.

III. Intervention Methods
- ◊ Directive/Supportive/ Problem Solving Approaches

IV. Strategies

> *** Obtain signed informed consent from the parents or legal guardian (clarify the limits of confidentiality in advance and include a clear financial/fee contract.)
> 1. To assess suicide-risk and danger to self and make appropriate intervention to secure safety of the child.
> 2. To assess the danger to others and make appropriate intervention.
> 3. Refer to M. D. for medical evaluation and medication intervention.
> 4. If child abuse is suspected, proceed with the necessary mandated report and protect the child's safety.

The Selected Mental Disorders in Children and Adolescents

> 5. If your client is a victim of abuse, proceed with the mandated child abuse report, and protect your client's safety. (Child/youth and family are considered a client)
> 6. Make intervention to deal with the immediate concern issues related to substance abuse.
> 7. Attend to the immediate concern (family or school related issues) crisis and contain it.
> 8. Attend to other immediate concern issues and make appropriate intervention.
> 9. Establish rapport with the child (be supportive, accepting and understanding, not judgmental) and establish alliance with child's family.

Short-Term Treatment Plan

I. Treatment Issues
- ◊ Defiant behavior
- ◊ Poor Self-control skills
- ◊ Agitation/anger
- ◊ Communication problems
- ◊ Use of inappropriate language with family members at home and at school
- ◊ Non compliant with appointment and treatment

II. Treatment Plan/Goals
- ◊ To decrease and contain symptomatic behavior/conduct.
- ◊ To improve coping skills/social skills.
- ◊ To deal with interactional problems at home and school caused by child's oppositional behavior.

III. Intervention Methods
- ◊ Supportive/Cognitive-Behavioral/psycho-educational Approaches

Oppositional Defiant Disorder

IV. Strategies

> 1. Use contingency management techniques to eliminate/decrease defiant behavior by recording defiant behavior, and parent's reaction to the child's behavior, and training parents on use of monitoring techniques, loss of privilege and using time-out for negative behavior, reinforcing positive behavior.
> 2. Improve self-control skills to contain problem behaviors.
> 3. Use self-monitoring techniques to manage agitation/anger.
> 4. Use self-monitoring techniques to eliminate use of inappropriate language.
> 5. Use role playing to improve communication in the family..
> 6. Provide reinforcement for positive interaction at home and school.
> 7. Cooperate with school to deal with academic problems.
> 8. Educate parents about the defiant behavior of the child..
> 9. If the child is depressed, refer for medication evaluation, and use cognitive-behavioral approach to deal with depression based on the child's age.
> 10. Provide incentive for child and parents to cooperate with the treatment recommendations.

Long-Term Treatment Plan

I. Treatment Issues
- ◊ Parental power struggle with child
- ◊ Communication/interaction problem in family
- ◊ Poor self-esteem
- ◊ Poor interpersonal skills

II. Treatment Plan/ Goals
- ◊ To deal with interaction problem of family.
- ◊ To deal with parental power struggle and rejection.
- ◊ To improve self-esteem.
- ◊ To prevent relapse of symptoms.

The Selected Mental Disorders in Children and Adolescents

III. Intervention Methods
- ◊ Supportive/ Cognitive-Behavioral/Family Therapy

IV. Strategies

1. Help client(child/youth) to identify positive things, behaviors and accomplishments about himself/herself in learning successful use of self-monitoring techniques) and improve positive self-concept (self-esteem)
2. To deal with parental power struggle, work with the family to <u>improve healthy communication</u>, not <u>over-pathologize child's behavior</u> and <u>change family's perception</u> of the child's behavior.
3. Help client to express and communicate his/her feelings of anger toward parents and rejection by parents.
4. To deal with interactional problems in the family, use role-playing, problem solving, and relaxation training to improve communication and interaction in family.
5. Continue self-monitoring techniques to maintain positive change, improvement and prevention from relapse.

Adjunct Treatment (Goals and Strategies)

1. Positive peer group for child (joining children or youth camp)
2. Participation in sports and activity group..
3. Support group for parents.

PART II

Application of Treatment Planning and Intervention:
The Selected Mental Disorders of Adults

Part II. Application of Treatment Planning and Intervention: The Selected Mental Health Disorders of Adults

Part II begins with the treatment of Adjustment Disorders. This part includes either a specific disorder such as Mood Disorder Due to General Medical Condition or a main category of the groups of disorders, such as Bipolar Disorder. Although a specific treatment approach is ideal for a specific mental disorder, taking into consideration the scope of this book, treatment planning for a main category relevant to a group of mental disorders is presented.

Part II includes treatment in three stages; immediate, short-term, and long-term plans are presented for the selected mental disorder or selected group of mental disorders. Included mental disorders in part II are Adjustment Disorder, Anxiety Disorder, Bipolar Disorder, Depressive Disorder, Eating Disorder, Mood Disorder Due to General Medical Condition, Posttraumatic Stress Disorder, Substance Use Disorder, and Schizophrenic Disorder.

The initial stage of the treatment plan is to address the immediate crisis and maintain the patient's safety. The second stage of the treatment plan emphasizes symptom reduction and prevention of the relapse of symptoms. A combined treatment approach with an emphasis on cognitive behavioral therapy and psycho-educational approaches with the option of medication intervention are considered for the second stage of the treatment intervention.

The last stage of the treatment plan described as a long-term plan of intervention emphasizes the intervention for long-lasting symptoms, personality features coexisting with the other signs and short-lasting symptoms, prevention of relapse into mental disorder in general, and improving the patient's level of functioning. At this stage of the treatment, supportive, psycho-educational, and insight-oriented treatment intervention approaches are considered to be effective in dealing with the long-lasting conditions and symptoms.

Adjustment Disorder

Immediate Treatment Plan

I. Treatment Issues
- Suicide-risk
- Child Abuse history
- Depressed mood
- Agitation
- Severe anxiety
- Dangerous to Others
- Exposure to extreme stressor
- Other life crisis

II. Treatment Plan/Goals
- To assess the severity of immediate concern issues and make appropriate intervention to contain the most severe and potentially dangerous condition.
- To assess stressor and contain its impact on the client.
- To proceed with the appropriate intervention to contain presented crisis and other immediate concern issues.

III. Intervention Methods
- Directive/Problem Solving/Supportive Approaches

IV. Strategies

> *** Obtain signed informed consent from the patient, parents or legal guardian, if patient is a child or minor (clarify the limits confidentiality in advance and include a clear financial/fee contract).
> 1. To assess suicide-risk and make necessary intervention.
> 2. To assess the danger to others and make appropriate intervention. proceed to file the mandated report if necessary.
> 3. Refer for medical evaluation and medication intervention.
> 4. Make appropriate intervention to deal with immediate concern issues related to substance abuse.

The Selected Mental Disorders of Adults

> 5. If he client is a victim of abuse, proceed with the mandated abuse report and protect the victim's safety.
> 6. Crisis intervention:
> - Immediate problem solving to contain major stressor.
> - Mobilize support system.
> - Help client to gain some control over his/her life.
> - Contain other sources of possible stressor (family/job).
> - Help client to contain and control negative emotions before they become overwhelming (consider holding frequent sessions to deal with negative emotions).

Short-Term Treatment Plan

I. Treatment Issues
- ◊ Anxiety
- ◊ Depressed mood
- ◊ Psychosomatic complications
- ◊ Sleep disturbance
- ◊ Fear
- ◊ Anger
- ◊ Rumination
- ◊ Poor concentration

II. Treatment Plan/Goals
- ◊ To reduce symptomatic behavior and eliminate symptoms.
- ◊ To change client's reaction towards stressors (stop rumination).
- ◊ To improve coping skills.

III. Intervention Methods
- ◊ Supportive/Cognitive-Behavioral/Psycho-educational Approaches

IV. Strategies
> 1. Establish working and therapeutic alliance with client.
> 2. Use Relaxation Training to deal with and reduce anxiety.
> 3. Use Cognitive Re-Structuring technique to reduce depression.
> 4. Help client to identify cognitive distortion causing the anxiety and fear and help client to change them.

Adjustment Disorder

> 5. Use thought stopping to deal with rumination.
> 6. Train client to use self-monitoring technique and stimulus control to deal with anxiety and sleep problems.
> 7. Educate client about the nature of his/her reaction to the stressor and help client to deal with anxiety effectively (consider using cognitive restructuring and relaxation techniques).
> 8. Use biofeedback technique to deal with psychosomatic complication if symptoms continue to resist
> 9. Improve coping skills (relaxation, assertiveness training, and using self-monitoring to prevent overwhelming anxiety related to stressors).
> 10. Foster and encourage client's compliance with the treatment intervention.

Long-Term Treatment Plan

I. Treatment Issues
- ◊ Sustained multiple stressors
- ◊ Impaired sense of control
- ◊ Low self-esteem
- ◊ Impaired social/vocational functioning

II. Treatment Plan/ Goals
- ◊ Prevent symptoms relapse.
- ◊ Deal with underlying issues of low self-esteem and impaired sense of control.
- ◊ Identify causes of stress-prone life style if there are continued multiple stressors and address life style change/improvement.

III. Intervention Methods
- ◊ Supportive/Insight Oriented /Cognitive Approaches/Any Appropriate Insight Oriented Therapy

The Selected Mental Disorders of Adults

IV. Strategies

1. Work with client and educate him/her to maintain recovery from symptoms and prevent relapse including substance abuse problem.
2. Work with client to identify the underlying issues of low self-esteem and impaired sense of self and challenge them.
3. Work with client to identify elements causing stressor prone life-style and change them effectively, if there are continued multiple stressors address life style changes and improvement.
4. Foster self-control in the patient in dealing with stressor.

Adjunct Treatment (Goals and Strategies)

1. Family therapy to deal with the impact of client's challenge with the stressor on the family.
2. Self-help group to share feelings about challenging stressors
3. Vocational counseling to deal with job-related issues such as maintaining a job.
4. AA or 12-step group if substance abuse is an issue.

Anxiety Disorder

Immediate Treatment Plan

I. Immediate Concern Treatment Issues
- ◊ Suicidality preoccupation
- ◊ Dangerous to others
- ◊ Dangerous to self
- ◊ Severe Anxiety
- ◊ Other Life Crisis
- ◊ Substance Abuse

II. Treatment Plan/Goals
- ◊ To assess the severity of immediate concern issues and to make appropriate intervention to contain the most severe conditions.
- ◊ To proceed with the appropriate intervention to contain presented crisis and other immediate concern issues.

III. Intervention Methods
- ◊ Directive/Problem Solving/Supportive Approaches

IV. Strategies

> *** Obtain signed informed consent for treatment (clarify the limits of confidentiality in advance and include a clear financial/fee contract.)
> 1. To assess and make intervention for suicide-risk and danger to self.
> 2. To assess the danger to others and make appropriate intervention. Proceed with mandated report if it s necessary.
> 3. Refer to M.D. for medical evaluation and medication intervention.
> 4. R/O general medical condition, organicity, and substance induced cause of anxiety if there is a lack of adequate supportive factors for Anxiety Disorder.
> 5. Make immediate intervention concerning substance abuse related condition (referral to detoxification).

The Selected Mental Disorders of Adults

> 6. Make intervention to reduce/eliminate immediate causes of anxiety (immediate problem solving to contain source of anxiety and mobilize support system if it is necessary).
> 7. Attend to the major presented crisis and proceed with taking action towards containing it.
> 8. Attend to other immediate concern issues and make appropriate intervention (i.e. child abuse, elder abuse, spousal abuse).

Short-Term Treatment Plan

I. Treatment Issues
- Anxiety
- Fear
- Hyper-vigilance
- Sleep problem
- Psychosomatic complications
- Interpersonal/job performance problem
- Poor coping skills to deal with common issues in daily life

II. Treatment Plan/Goals
- To reduce and eliminate anxiety and other symptomatic behaviors and conditions.
- To improve coping skills.
- To deal with interpersonal/job performance problem related to severe anxiety.

III. Intervention Methods
- Supportive/Cognitive-Behavioral/Psycho-educational Approaches

IV. Strategies
> 1. Establish working and therapeutic alliance with client.
> 2. Educate client about the cause and nature of his/her anxiety and how anxiety is affecting his/her life.

Anxiety Disorder

> 3. Use Systematic Desensitization in Panic D.O., Social Phobia, Simple Phobia, Agoraphobia, and Generalized Anxiety D.O.
> 4. Use cognitive re-structuring technique to deal with fear and anxiety in Obsessive-Compulsive D.O., and other anxiety disorders.
> 5. Use Relaxation Training technique to deal with anxiety and hyper-vigilance.
> 6. Use Implosive Therapy techniques to deal with anxiety in Agoraphobia, Social phobia and Simple Phobia.
> 7. Use Biofeedback techniques to deal with psychosomatic complications.
> 8. Train client to use Self Monitoring and Stimulus Control techniques to deal with anxiety and sleep complications.
> 9. Improve Coping Skills (Relaxation Training, Assertiveness Training and Self Monitoring).
> 10. Problem solving and Psycho-educational intervention to deal with job related issues (taking time off, reducing hours).
> 11. Foster and encourage client's compliance with treatment intervention.

Long-Term Treatment Plan

I. Treatment Issues
- ◊ Fear of having anxiety attack
- ◊ Impaired sense of control
- ◊ Early life rejection
- ◊ Impaired self-esteem
- ◊ Job performance difficulty
- ◊ Family relationship problem caused by client's condition.

II. Treatment Plan/ Goals
- ◊ To prevent relapse.
- ◊ To deal with underlying issues of fear, rejection by others and sense of control.
- ◊ To improve self-esteem.

The Selected Mental Disorders of Adults

III. Intervention Methods
 ◊ Supportive/ Cognitive-Behavioral/Insight Oriented Approaches

IV. Strategies

> 1. To help client to maintain recovery and prevent from relapse of symptomatic behavior and condition.
> 2. To work with client to identify the underlying issues/causes of fear, impaired sense of self, and impaired sense of control, and deal with them effectively.
> 3. To identify the underlying causes of anxiety, interpret them, and educate client about the nature of his/her anxiety.
> 4. Improve self-esteem and self-control by identifying <u>positive progress in treatment, maintaining recovery, and client's accomplishment</u> in controlling anxiety and other disturbing symptoms.
> 5. Encourage client to practice recommended homework, and follow-up with client in handling of residual anxiety condition.
> 6. Encourage client in his/her efforts in dealing with disturbing mental health condition.

Adjunct Treatment (Goals and Strategies)

> 1. Family Therapy (to deal with the family problem related to the client's anxiety complication).
> 2. Group Therapy (Support and Growth group).
> 3. To encourage client to join a Health and Social Club to improve his/her social skills.
> 4. Vocational Counseling to deal with job-related issues.
> 5. AA group participation, if substance abuse is an issue.
> 6. Critical to fostering a healthy and positive life style, encourage client to join healthy social clubs, attend skill training classes and practice sporting activities.

Bipolar Disorder

Immediate Treatment Plan

I. Immediate Concern Treatment Issues
- Suicide-risk
- Dangerous to others
- Dangerous to self
- Manic episodes
- Severe mood swings
- Other Life Crisis
- Substance abuse

II. Treatment Plan/Goals
- To assess the severity of immediate concern issues and to make appropriate intervention to contain the most severe and potentially dangerous conditions.
- To proceed with the appropriate intervention to contain presented crisis and other immediate concern issues.

III. Intervention Methods
- Directive/Problem Solving/Supportive Approaches

IV. Strategies

*** Obtain signed informed consent for treatment (clarify the limits confidentiality in advance and include a clear financial/fee contract.)
1. To assess and make intervention for suicide-risk and danger to self.
2. To assess the danger to others and make appropriate intervention. Proceed with mandated report if necessary.
3. Refer to M.D. for medical evaluation and medication intervention.
4. R/O diagnosis, due to G.M.C, substance induced causes prior to proceeding to specific intervention for Bipolar Disorder.
5. Consider hospitalization if client is experiencing severe manic condition.
6. Make intervention to deal with immediate concern issues of substance abuse.
7. Attend to other immediate concern issues (Child abuse).

The Selected Mental Disorders of Adults

> 8. Attend to the other life crisis and proceed with intervention to contain it.
> 9. Mobilize support system for providing support and help to client.

Short-Term Treatment Plan

I. Treatment Issues:
- ◊ Denial of mental health condition
- ◊ Resistant to intervention for stabilization
- ◊ Anxiety
- ◊ Irritability and unstable mood with elation
- ◊ Agitation
- ◊ Sleep problem
- ◊ Impulsivity
- ◊ Pressured speech
- ◊ Poor judgment

II. Treatment Plan/Goals
- ◊ To deal with denial of mental health condition and resistance to treatment.
- ◊ To reduce and eliminate symptoms and other symptomatic behaviors and conditions.
- ◊ To improve coping skills and poor judgment.

III. Intervention Methods
- ◊ Supportive/Cognitive-Behavioral/Psycho-educational Approaches

IV. Strategies

> 1. Establish working and therapeutic alliance with client (Be empathetic to his/her feelings).
> 2. Deal with client's denial about of mental health condition and resistance to treatment (educate client about the cause, effect and nature of his/her illness on his/her life and the positive effect of treatment).
> 3. Train client to use self monitoring to deal with impulsivity.

Bipolar Disorder

> 4. Train client to use relaxation exercise to reduce anxiety, irritability and agitation.
> 5. Use Relaxation Training technique to deal with sleep problem and irritability.
> 6. Practice reality testing exercises to deal with client's judgment and planning/decision-making problems.
> 7. Improve Coping Skills to deal with daily living issues and emotional/mental condition (communicating his/her needs, being assertive but not demanding) using self-monitoring and relaxation which are very effective.
> 8. Use modeling and rehearsal to deal with speech problem.
> 9. Consider referring client for a comprehensive psychological testing for follow-up planning and intervention.

Long-Term Treatment Plan

I. Treatment Issues
- Poor sense of self control
- Expansive sense of self concept
- Resistance to treatment and follow-up
- Fear of being mentally ill
- Poor adaptive social skills
- Impaired social/vocational functioning

II. Treatment Plan/ Goals
- To prevent relapse.
- To deal with issue of self-control and self-concept.
- To deal with fears/resistance to treatment.
- To deal with family/social/vocational problems caused by mental health condition.

III. Intervention Methods
- Supportive/ Directive/Cognitive-Behavioral/Insight Oriented Approaches

The Selected Mental Disorders of Adults

IV. Strategies

1. Use psycho-educational approach to help client to stay in therapy to prevent relapse and maintain adequate level of stabilization.
2. Deal with client's fears and resistance to treatment, review <u>improvement of client's condition</u> and recovery towards stabilization.
3. To help client to improve his/her sense of control by controlling his/her illness.
4. Deal with interpersonal issues affecting client's family/social/vocational functioning, and challenge them in therapy.
5. Encourage client in his/her effort in dealing with challenging mental health condition.

Adjunct Treatment (Goals and Strategies)

1. Family therapy to deal with issues of the client's mental condition affecting the family relationship and family functioning.
2. Group Therapy (Support and Growth group).
3. Vocational Counseling to deal with job-related issues.
4. AA or any type of substance abuse prevention support group is recommended.

Depressive Disorder

Immediate Treatment Plan

I. Immediate Concern Treatment Issues
- ◊ Suicide-risk
- ◊ Dangerous to self
- ◊ Lack of Support System
- ◊ Feeling of helplessness/hopelessness
- ◊ Other Life Crisis including childhood abuse history
- ◊ Depressive episodes
- ◊ Psychotic symptoms in some cases
- ◊ Substance abuse problem

II. Treatment Plan/Goals
- ◊ To assess the severity of immediate concern issues and to make appropriate intervention to contain the most severe and potentially dangerous condition.
- ◊ To assess current stressor and crisis and proceed with appropriate intervention to contain presented stressor, crisis and other immediate concern issues.

III. Intervention Methods
- ◊ Directive/Problem Solving/Supportive Approaches

IV. Strategies

> *** Obtain signed informed consent for treatment (clarify the limits confidentiality in advance and include a clear financial/fee contract.)
> 1. To assess and make necessary intervention do deal with suicide-risk and danger to self.
> 2. Consider hospitalization if client is experiencing severe depression and he/she is potentially dangerous to self.
> 3. Refer to M.D. for medical evaluation and medication intervention.
> 4. R/O diagnosis, due to G.M.C, organicity and substance induced causes prior to proceeding to specific intervention for Depressive Disorder.
> 5. Make intervention to deal with immediate concern issues of substance abuse.

The Selected Mental Disorders of Adults

> 6. Make intervention to reduce depressed mood, and feeling of hopelessness/helplessness by being empathetic, supporting and <u>offering effective problem solving</u> to address the needs of the client.
> 7. Mobilize support system, <u>or</u> refer the client to a safe and supportive environment for short-term placement.
> 8. Attend to the other life crisis and proceed with intervention to contain it.
> 9. Attend to other immediate concern issues and make appropriate intervention (victim of abusive relationship, victim of assault).

Short-Term Treatment Plan

   I. Treatment Issues
- Depressed mood
- Suicide preoccupation (transient)
- Apathy
- Psychomotor retardation or agitation
- Low energy
- Sleep disturbance
- Low self esteem
- Sense of helplessness/hopelessness
- Disturbed appetite
- Fear of giving up to depression
- Psychotic symptoms in some cases

   II. Treatment Plan/Goals
- To reduce and eliminate severe depressive conditions and symptoms related to depressive disorder.
- To improve coping skills.
- Prevention from relapse into suicide-risk behavior and danger to self.

   III. Intervention Methods
- Supportive/Directive/Cognitive-Behavioral/Psycho-educational Approaches

Depressive Disorder

IV. Strategies

> 1. Establish working and therapeutic alliance with client.
> 2. Consider on-going suicide-risk assessment as it is necessary for client's safety.
> 3. Educate client about the nature and cause of depressive condition and symptoms, how they affect his/her life, and how treatment will help to improve his/her condition.
> 4. Use Cognitive Restructuring technique to deal with negative thoughts, sense of helplessness/hopelessness and low self esteem.
> 5. Train client to use Self Monitoring Technique to monitor negative thoughts and distorted thoughts/feelings.
> 6. Train client to use Self Monitoring and Stimulus Control Techniques to deal with sleep problem.
> 7. Train client to use Self Monitoring Technique to normalize eating schedule and pattern.
> 8. Work with client in developing an Activity Schedule and monitoring Mastering Pleasure Rating to improve level of functioning and energy.
> 9. Encourage client in practicing homework on Mastery Pleasure Rating.
> 10. Improve coping skills (relaxation and assertiveness training), communicating his/her needs, using self monitoring on practicing coping skills.
> 11. Consider referring client for a comprehensive psychological testing for follow-up planning and intervention.

Long-Term Treatment Plan

I. Treatment Issues
- ◊ Depressive mood
- ◊ Low self esteem
- ◊ Suicide preoccupation, ideation (transient)
- ◊ Excessive guilt feeling
- ◊ Sense of worthlessness
- ◊ Preoccupation with early life trauma issues
- ◊ Weight problem (under/overweight)

The Selected Mental Disorders of Adults

- ◊ Impaired social, vocational functioning
- ◊ Psychotic symptoms in some cases

II. Treatment Plan/ Goals
- ◊ To prevent relapse of suicidal symptom and depressive episode.
- ◊ To deal with underlying issues guilt, low self esteem and sense of worthlessness.
- ◊ To deal with weight problem.
- ◊ To improve positive and constructive thinking and feelings about himself/herself.
- ◊ To improve family and social relationships, and vocational functioning.

III. Intervention Methods
- ◊ Directive/Insight Oriented/Supportive/Psycho-educational Approaches

IV. Strategies

1. Work with client to stay in therapy to prevent from relapse and maintain adequate level of stabilization.
2. Perform ongoing assessment for suicide-risk.
3. Work with client to explore and identify the underlying issues of guilt-feelings, sense of worthlessness and low self esteem. Clarify, interpret, and challenge some of the client's negative beliefs when it is appropriate (watch for suicidality).
4. Deal with the early life trauma issues affecting client's depressive condition, parental rejection, child abuse in early life and loss of loved one.
5. Continue working with client on using Self Monitoring techniques to normalize eating pattern and schedule. Encourage client to see M.D. for malnutrition problems.
6. Deal with interpersonal problem affecting client's family and social, life and his/her vocational functioning. Identify issues and challenge them in therapy.
7. Deal effectively with the problems related to therapy termination in time, develop a practical follow-up plan and prepare client in advance for termination.

Depressive Disorder

Adjunct Treatment (Goals and Strategies)

1. Family therapy to deal with resistance in the family for change and improvement in client's condition.
2. Group Therapy (Support and Growth group).
3. Continue Assertiveness Training
4. Vocational counseling to deal with job-related problems.
5. Nutritional counseling to deal with weight problem.
6. AA/Daul Diag. group if substance abuse is an issue.
7. For fostering healthy and positive life style, participation in skill training classes, joining health/social/sport clubs to improve client's interpersonal/social skills is critical.

Eating Disorder

Immediate Treatment Plan/Goals

I. Immediate Concern Treatment Issues
- ◊ Danger to Self
- ◊ Suicide Risk
- ◊ Weight loss
- ◊ Serious medical condition
- ◊ Substance Abuse
- ◊ Child abuse history
- ◊ Other Crisis

II. Treatment Plan/Goals
- ◊ To assess the severity of immediate concern issues and make appropriate intervention to contain the most severe and potentially dangerous condition.
- ◊ To proceed with the appropriate intervention to contain the presented crisis and other immediate concern issues.

III. Intervention Methods/Approaches
- ◊ Directive/ Problem Solving/Supportive Approaches

IV. Strategies

> *** Obtain a signed informed consent form from an adult. Clarify the limits of confidentiality and obtain a signed informed consent from parents or legal guardian if client is a minor for treatment. (Include a clear financial/fee contract).
> 1. Assess and make appropriate intervention to deal with dangerousness to self.
> 2. Refer to M.D. for medical evaluation, medication intervention and regulating eating routine.
> 3. Consider hospitalization if necessary due to client's condition.
> 4. Make immediate intervention related to substance abuse related condition (referral to detox).

The Selected Mental Disorders of Adults

> 5. Attend to the major presented crisis and proceed with taking action to contain it.
> 6. Attend to other immediate concern issues and make appropriate intervention (i.e. child abuse).

Short-Term Treatment Plan

I. Treatment Issues
- ◊ Medical complication
- ◊ Depression
- ◊ Anxiety
- ◊ Obsession with body weight
- ◊ Interpersonal problem issues affecting therapeutic relationship
- ◊ Sleep Problems
- ◊ Dangerous to self
- ◊ Non compliance with treatment and feeding intervention
- ◊ Relational problem with immediate support system (parents, spouse)

II. Treatment Plan/Goals
- ◊ To restore normal eating behavior.
- ◊ To facilitate weight restoration.
- ◊ To reduce and eliminate symptomatic behaviors.
- ◊ To deal with interpersonal problems/therapeutic relationship.
- ◊ To intervene in client's relationship problem with support system.

III. Intervention Methods/Approaches
- ◊ Supportive/Behavioral and Cognitive/psycho-educational Approaches

IV. Strategies
> 1. Establish working and therapeutic alliance with client about eating problem (Not challenging client about eating, be empathetic about client's feelings).
> 2. Cooperate with M.D. and work with client to support follow up medical treatment for physical/medical complication due to eating disorder.
> 3. Ongoing assessment of possible danger to self and providing intervention if necessary.

Eating Disorder

> 4. Educate client about the nature of his/her illness and positive outcome of the treatment.
> 5. Make a contract with client to normalize his/her eating pattern (regular eating schedule/certain number of meals daily).
> 6. Apply Self Monitoring Technique to monitor eating (improves sense of self control).
> 7. To restore body weight, normalize exercise (apply Stimulus Control Technique, setting limits on time, types and location of exercise).
> 8. Normalize sleep (Use relaxation technique, Stimulus Control, and Self Monitoring Techniques and thought stopping)
> 9. Use Cognitive Restructuring Technique to deal with client's extreme concern and obsession about <u>Body Image</u> and weight.
> 10. Use Cognitive Restructuring Technique to deal with depression and anxiety.
> 11. Use Biofeedback Techniques to intervene and deal with psychosomatic nature of eating disorder.
> 12. Improve coping skills (Relaxation, Assertiveness Training).
> 13. Motivate/educate client about getting nutritional counseling.

Long-Term Treatment Plan

I. Treatment Issues
- ◊ Dependency
- ◊ Perfectionism tendency
- ◊ Low self esteem
- ◊ Anger
- ◊ Interpersonal relationship problem and boundary issue in family

II. Treatment Plan/ Goals
- ◊ To prevent relapse.
- ◊ To challenge perfectionism in therapy.
- ◊ To improve self esteem.
- ◊ To improve/normalize boundary issue in family.
- ◊ Deal with anger.

The Selected Mental Disorders of Adults

III. Intervention Methods/Approaches
- ◊ Cognitive-Behavioral /Insight Oriented/Directive/ Supportive Approaches (Family/Individual Therapy)

IV. Strategies

1. To help client to take responsibility to maintain recovery (regulate food intake, normalize exercise and follow up the treatment).
2. To help client to identify positive things about the self and improve self concept (identifying recovery success).
3. Deal with underlying issues related to anger, dependency and perfectionism (identifying, interpreting, clarifying).
4. Family therapy using Minuchin's Structural Approach to deal with boundary issues, overprotectiveness/rigidity in family and emotional partner relationship.
**5. (If client is a minor) Help family to identify the dysfunctional family structure and modify it by addressing <u>sick role</u> of minor in family, <u>triangulation</u>, and <u>concealing marital problem</u>.
6. Family lunch to determine schedule for parents acting jointly to encourage the minor to eat (changing eating environment).

Adjunct Treatment (Goals and Strategies)

1. Nutritional counseling
2. Group therapy
3. Support Group
4. Assertiveness training
5. AA or NA group if substance abuse is an issue.

Mood Disorder Due to General Medical Condition

Immediate Treatment Plan/Goals

I. Immediate Concern Treatment Issues
- ◊ Suicide Risk
- ◊ Major medical condition
- ◊ Depressed mood in depressed type
- ◊ Slowed thinking in depressed type
- ◊ Distractibility in manic type
- ◊ Possible danger to others in manic type
- ◊ Irritability elevated or expansive mood in manic type
- ◊ Danger to self
- ◊ Feeling of helplessness
- ◊ Medication abuse
- ◊ Anxiety

II. Treatment Plan/Goals
- ◊ To assess the severity of immediate concern issues/crisis and make appropriate intervention to maintain the client's safety.
- ◊ To assess other concern issues and proceed with appropriate intervention to contain presented condition and other immediate concern issues.

III. Intervention Methods
- ◊ Directive/ Problem Solving/Supportive Approaches

IV. Strategies

> *** Obtain signed informed consent from the parents or legal guardian if patient is a minor (clarify the limits confidentiality in advance and include a clear financial/fee contract.)
> 1. Be alert if the condition of the patient indicates medical emergency and take appropriate action to secure safety of the patient (calling emergency, use of hospital/ambulance, emergency call to patient's physician).

The Selected Mental Disorders of Adults

> 2. Proceed with hospitalization process as soon as possible and be alert to suicidality and danger to self.
> 3. Assess suicide risk and danger to self and make appropriate intervention.
> 4. Assess potential danger to others and make appropriate intervention. If necessary, proceed with the mandated report.
> 5. Cooperate with the physician and medical staff by maintaining stability of patient's emotional condition in response to his/her medical condition.
> 6. Refer to M.D. for medication intervention if it is necessary for very depressed mood, sever anxiety and irritability.
> 7. Provide direct and supportive intervention to reduce depressed mood and feeling of helplessness by being empathetic and supportive.
> 8. Attend to other immediate concern issues and crises and contain the adverse effects on client.
> 9. Mobilize support systems for providing support and help to client.
> 10. Help client to use breathing and relaxation techniques to reduce anxiety and irritability caused by a G.M.C.
> 11. Be alert for patient's medication abuse and make appropriate intervention.

Short-Term Treatment Plan

   I. Treatment Issues
- High risk of danger to self
- Depression
- Non compliance with medical treatment
- Depressed concerns about basic nutrition and poor appetite
- Extensive anxiety about the medical condition/problem
- Sleep disturbance
- Agitation/irritability
- Elevated/expansive mood in manic type
- Limited awareness of limits of progress of medical condition in manic type
- Depressed mood in depressed type
- Psychomotor retardation in depressed type
- Feeling of helplessness in depressed type

Mood Disorder Due to General Medical Condition

II. Treatment Plan/Goals
- ◊ To deal with noncompliance behavior towards medical intervention and treatment.
- ◊ To reduce/eliminate psychological symptomatic behaviors caused by medical condition.
- ◊ To improve coping skills in dealing with medical/psychological condition.

III. Intervention Methods
- ◊ Supportive/Cognitive-Behavioral/psycho-educational Approaches

IV. Strategies
1. Establish working and therapeutic alliance with client (Be empathetic about client's feelings and needs).
2. To deal with non-compliance with medical treatment, cooperate with medical team and educate client about his/her medical condition/emotional condition and process of the progress.
3. Cooperate with the medical team and nutritionist to educate client about his/her physical/emotional condition that affects his/her appetite and nutrition. Train client to use self-monitoring technique to normalize eating pattern.
4. To cooperate with the medical team, educate the client about the <u>process of progress and possible limits</u> of medical physical condition.
5. Lower anxiety, (a) cooperating with medical team in educating client about his/her medical condition and the process of progress and recovery. (b) training client to use <u>breathing</u> and <u>relaxation exercises</u> daily.
6. Train client to use self monitoring, stimulus control technique and relaxation exercise to deal with sleep problem.
7. Train client to use self monitoring technique to reduce agitation and irritability.
8. Use Cognitive Re-structuring Technique to deal wth negative thoughts and sense of helplessness to decrease depressed mood.
9. Work with client to develop appropriate activity schedule to improve his/her functioning level and mood stabilization.

The Selected Mental Disorders of Adults

> 10. Improve coping skills by training client to use relaxation exercise, assertiveness training, and communicating his/her needs and feelings.
> 11. Consider a referral for comprehensive psychological testing.

Long-Term Treatment Plan

   I. Treatment Issues
- ◊ Transient suicidal condition due to medical complication
- ◊ Low self esteem/sense of worthlessness.
- ◊ Complication from treatment follow up
- ◊ Impaired social/vocational functioning due to medical condition
- ◊ Anger/frustration caused by limitation of physical condition
- ◊ Fear of further complication with medical condition

   II. Treatment Plan/Goals
- ◊ To prevent relapse of suicidality and emotional complication due to G.M.C.
- ◊ To maintain treatment for medical condition.
- ◊ To improve poor sense of control and low self esteem.
- ◊ To improve self esteem.
- ◊ To deal with fears about medical condition.
- ◊ To deal with emotional trauma caused by medical condition.
- ◊ To help client to develop a more realistic concept and picture of his/her medical complication. Help client to be aware of and understand the concept and association he/she has developed about conditions of the medical complications.
- ◊ To deal with family/social/vocational problems caused by his/her medical complication a d emotional response to this complication.

   III. Intervention Methods
- ◊ Supportive/Directive/Supportive/Psycho-educational/Insight Oriented Approaches

Mood Disorder Due to General Medical Condition

IV. Strategies

1. Work with client, using Psycho-educational approach to help him/her to maintain reception of medical care and prevent medical condition relapse.
2. Help client to remain in therapy intervention to prevent from relapse of mental health symptoms and potential suicidality.
3. Maintain the safety of the therapeutic relationship by empathizing with the client about medical condition and help him/her to alter the sense of self control and control the symptoms.
4. Review with client about the improved status and progress in dealing with his/her medical condition.
5. Help client to change the inner sense and concept of his/her medical complication by examining and differentiating the real properties and elements of the medical complication from the inner concept about that condition.
6. Deal with the traumatic effect of the medical complication on his/her relationship with family/spouse, social and vocational functioning.

Adjunct Treatment (Goals and Strategies)

1. Family/couple therapy to address how client's medical complication and his/her mental health condition affecting family functioning and relationships.
2. Support group participation with individuals who have similar medical complication.
3. Encourage client to join health club to improve his/her health life style.
4. Refer to nutritional counseling to address healthy eating habits
5. Refer to substance abuse support group if medication abuse is an issue.
6. Group therapy to maintain work on problem caused by on-going medical condition.
7. For fostering a healthy and positive life style, encouraging client to join healthy social clubs, skill training classes, and participation in sports are critical.

Posttraumatic Stress Disorder

Immediate Treatment Plan/Goals

I. Immediate Concern Treatment Issues
- Suicide preoccupation
- Excessive anxiety
- Depressed mood
- Cognitive Distortion
- Other life crisis
- Past trauma
- Dangerous to self
- Dangerous to others
- Substance abuse problem

II. Treatment Plan/Goals
- To assess the severity of the immediate concern issues and current crisis to make necessary intervention to maintain client's safety.
- To assess current stressors, other crisis, and related issues to proceed with the appropriate intervention to contain stressors, crisis and other immediate concern issues.

III. Intervention Methods
- Directive/ Problem Solving/Supportive Approaches

IV. Strategies

*** Obtain signed informed consent for treatment (clarify the limits of confidentiality in advance and include a clear financial/fee contract.)
1. To assess the severity of dangerousness to self and suicide-risk and proceed with the necessary intervention. To consider 72-hours Hospitalization if suicide risk is high.
2. To assess the danger to others and make necessary and appropriate intervention. Proceed with mandated report if it is necessary.
3. If suspected of child abuse trauma, proceed with the mandated Child Abuse report and protect client from further victimization.

4. Refer to M.D. for medical evaluation and medication intervention.
5. Make direct intervention to eliminate, contain, or reduce the impact of the immediate stressor.
6. Make direct intervention to reduce and contain severe anxiety (containing the immediate sources of anxiety, effective problem solving intervention, induction of relaxation exercise, and breathing exercise.)
7. Make immediate intervention concerning substance abuse problem (Immediate referral to detoxification if it is necessary).
8. Attend to the crisis related to the flashback experience of the past trauma. Encourage patient to verbalize his/her thoughts and feelings.
9. Attend to other immediate concern issues and make appropriate intervention (elder abuse, spousal abuse, or other types of abuse). Proceed with the necessary and mandated reports.
10. Mobilize support system for providing support and help to client.
11. Consider hospitalization if a client presents multiple severe symptoms including severe depression, vague auditory hallucinations, severe anxiety, and a potential danger to others.

Short-Term Treatment Plan

I. Treatment Issues
- ◊ Transient Suicidal ideation
- ◊ Anxiety/Depression
- ◊ Hyper-vigilance
- ◊ Fear
- ◊ Rumination
- ◊ Cognitive distortion
- ◊ Flashback
- ◊ Preoccupation with trauma
- ◊ Sleep disturbance
- ◊ Psychosomatic complication
- ◊ Problem with job and daily functioning due to unstable emotion

II. Treatment Plan/Goals
- ◊ To deal with suicidal thoughts and prevent from self-harm behavior.
- ◊ To reduce and eliminate symptomatic conditions.
- ◊ To alter maladaptive responses to the past trauma incident.
- ◊ To improve coping, relaxation, and stress management skills.

Posttraumatic Stress Disorder

III. Intervention Methods
◊ Directive/Supportive/Cognitive-Behavioral/Psycho-educational Approaches

IV. Strategies

1. Establish working and therapeutic alliance with client. (Be empathic to clients feelings about his/her past trauma.)
2. Educate client about his/her mental health condition and help him/her to identify his/her strengths helping to regain some control of his/ her own world.
3. Consider on-going suicide-risk assessment as it is necessary for client's safety and for prevention from self-harm behavior.
4. Use relaxation to deal with anxiety and reduce hyper-vigilance.
5. Normalize sleep (Use relaxation technique, Stimulus Control, and Self-Monitoring Techniques and thought stopping)
6. Educate client about symptoms of anxiety, depression and hyper-vigilance as his/her secondary response to trauma. Help client to gain some control in using self-monitoring techniques if emotional responses (i.e ; fear) are overwhelming.
7. Use Systematic Desensitization to deal with the stimuli associated with the traumatic experience. This helps flashback reduction.
8. Use Cognitive Restructuring Techniques to reduce <u>obsessive preoccupation</u> about the trauma.
9. Use Cognitive Restructuring Techniques to deal with <u>cognitive distortion</u> related to the trauma.
10. Use Assertiveness Training and problem solving skills to improve coping skills and basic stress management skills for prevention from symptoms relapses.
11. Consider a referral for a comprehensive psychological testing prior to termination of Short-Term Treatment to assess symptoms status.
12. Work with client to develop a positive and normal daily activity schedule to improve the level of functioning.

The Selected Mental Disorders of Adults

> 13. Encourage client to take active role in practicing daily schedule. If client indicates preoccupation in maintaining a sick role, proceed with the therapeutic challenging of sick role tendencies.

Long-Term Treatment Plan

I. Treatment Issues:
- ◊ Impaired sense of self-control
- ◊ Low self- esteem
- ◊ Latent flashbacks about trauma
- ◊ Fear
- ◊ Guilt feeling
- ◊ Self blame
- ◊ Distorted view of the trauma
- ◊ other early life traumas
- ◊ Impaired social/vocational functioning

II. Treatment Plan/ Goals
- ◊ To prevent from relapse of symptoms.
- ◊ To reduce client's distorted view of the past trauma affecting his/her current daily functioning.
- ◊ To intervene with client's self- blame, fear, and guilt feeling.
- ◊ To help client to develop a more realistic concept of current/ recent stressors and the world around him/her.
- ◊ To intervene with client's impaired sense of self control.
- ◊ To intervene with possible and further exposure to other life trauma that might trigger a relapse of the recovered symptoms.

III. Intervention Methods
- ◊ Directive/Supportive/Cognitive-Behavioral/Insight Oriented/Psycho-educational Approaches.

Posttraumatic Stress Disorder

IV. Strategies

1. To educate client about the process of recovery to help him/her staying in treatment till adequate level of stabilization build up gradually.
2. To maintain the safety of the therapeutic relationship by empathizing with client's in helping him to alter the status of self-control, and controlling the symptoms.
3. Review with client about his/her accomplishment made in therapy in helping client to regain an adaptive and positive sense of self- esteem.
4. To help client to alter the inner sense and concept about recent/current stressors by examining and differentiating the real properties and elements of the stressors from the inner and unreal concepts that client had formed based on past trauma experiences.
5. To help client to identify and explore the underlying issues of guilt feeling, fears, and self-blame related to the past trauma. Proceed with clarification, interpret and challenge some of the beliefs when appropriate. (Be alert about transient suicidal ideation and intervene for prevention possible unexpected acting on suicidal ideation.)
6. Deal with other issues of early life trauma and recent trauma related elements affecting client's current mental health condition and functioning. Help client to be aware of the associations he/she had developed between unrelated traumas or element related to traumas.
7. Deal with client's impaired social functioning (varies for different clients). Help client making improvement in this area. Referral for adjunct treatment is very critical.
8. Deal effectively with the issues related to therapy termination in time. Prepare client in advance for therapy termination and develop a practical follow-up plan.

Adjunct Treatment (Goals and Strategies)

1. Family/Couple therapy to address the impact of client's mental health condition on relationship with spouse, life partner, and family members.
2. Encourage client to enroll in support group for PTSD clients.

The Selected Mental Disorders of Adults

3. Refer client to substance abuse support group if he/she has a history of substance abuse related or not related to trauma.
4. Refer client to group therapy on self-esteem, coping skills and stress management skills in helping client to maintain his/her improved condition and helping client with stabilization.
5. Refer client for Vocational counseling.
6. For purpose of fostering positive and healthy life style, enrollment in social and interpersonal skill training classes, healthy social clubs, and joining sport clubs are helpful.

Substance Use Disorder

Short-Term Treatment Plan

I. Immediate Concern Treatment Issues
- Intoxication
- Dangerous to self
- Medical complication due to substance abuse
- Suicide-risk
- Childhood abuse history
- Dangerous to others
- Spouse/Life Partner abuse
- Elder abuse
- Other life Crisis
- Psychotic symptoms in some cases

II. Treatment Plan/Goals
- To assess the most severe immediate concern issues/crisis and to make appropriate intervention to deal and maintain the client's safety.
- To assess the other concerned crisis and issues and proceed with appropriate intervention to contain the other immediate concern issues and presented condition.

III. Intervention Methods/Approaches
- Directive/Problem Solving/Supportive Approaches

IV. Strategies

*** Obtain signed informed consent for treatment and intervention (clarify the limits of confidentiality in advance and include a clear financial/fee contract).
1. To assess and manage the necessary intervention to deal with suicide-risk and danger to self.
2. To assess the danger to others and make appropriate intervention. Proceed with mandated report if necessary.
3. Be alert if the patient's substance abuse requires medical emergency. Take appropriate action to secure the patient's safety.

4. Initiate referral for detoxification if necessary.
5. Deal with client's denial to get detoxed (family meeting, confronting patient, helping client to identify the adverse behaviors due to substance abuse problem.
6. Refer to M.D. for medical evaluation and medication intervention.
7. Consider hospitalization if it is necessary due to client's medical condition.
8. If suspected child abuse, knowledge of elder or dependent abuse, proceed with the necessary report and initiate intervention to protect the safety of victims.
9. Attend to the other life crises and contain it.
10. Attend to other immediate concern issues and make appropriate intervention.
11. Mobilize support system for providing support and help to client.

Short-Term Treatment Plan

I. Treatment Issues
- Relapse of substance abuse
- Dangerous to self due to substance abuse
- Depression
- Agitation
- Sleep problem
- Noncompliance with treatment
- Poor coping skills to deal with daily life stresses
- Psychotic symptoms in some cases

II. Treatment Plan/Goals
- To maintain sober living, prevent from relapse.
- To reduce and eliminate symptomatic behaviors and conditions.
- To improve coping skills.

III. Intervention Methods/Approaches
- Supportive/Cognitive-Behavioral/Psycho-educational Approaches

Substance Use Disorder

IV. Strategies

1. Make a contract with client to stay sober.
2. Deal with client's refusal to treatment (confronting client, reminding client of consequences of substance abuse as it is appropriate).
3. Educate client to use Self Monitoring Technique to deal with intention/desire to drink.
4. Educate client abut recovery process and relapse.
5. Relapse prevention training (educate client of the danger of substance abuse, and possibility of relapse, avoiding situation where substance is available).
6. To deal with guilt feeling and failure if relapse occurs. (Use cognitive restructuring technique.)
7. Use cognitive restructuring approach to deal with negative thoughts and beliefs related to depression coexisting with substance abuse problem.
8. Train client to use Self Monitoring, Stimulus Control, and Relaxation exercise to deal with sleep problem.
9. Improve Coping Skills to deal with daily stress (use relaxation, anger management, assertiveness training).
10. Train client to develop appropriate activity schedule to improve his/her life functioning level.
11. (In-patient treatment: Token Economy and Covert Sensitization are very appropriate and effective approaches).
12. Consider a referral for a comprehensive psychological testing.

Long-Term Treatment Plan

I. Treatment Issues
- ◊ Dependency
- ◊ Depressed Mood
- ◊ Impulsivity
- ◊ Parental rejection
- ◊ Poor self control
- ◊ Relapse
- ◊ Interpersonal/relational problems (spouse/family/others)

The Selected Mental Disorders of Adults

- ◊ Impaired social/vocational functioning
- ◊ Psychotic symptoms in some cases

II. Treatment Plan/Goals
- ◊ To prevent relapse.
- ◊ To deal with underlying issue of family rejection, interpersonal problems and dependency in relationships (long-term treatment may be necessary if other conditions exist, e.g. depression).
- ◊ To deal with family/social/vocational problems and develop a plan for improvement.
- ◊ To deal with poor self-control and impulsivity.

III. Intervention Methods/Approaches
- ◊ Directive/Psycho-educational/Supportive/Cognitive-Behavioral/Insight Oriented/Approaches

IV. Strategies

1. Help client to take responsibility to maintain sober living and follow-up intervention.
2. Help client to identify the underlying issues related to dependency and feeling of rejection by his/her parents. (Deal with these issues using insight-oriented approach).
3. Deal with family dysfunction affecting the client's progress and improvement.
4. Deal with client's defenses and transference affecting treatment progress (Identifying, interpreting, confrontation).
5. Using directive approach, deal with interpersonal/job related issues (reducing work hours, dealing with communication).
6. Continue using self-monitoring in dealing with impulsivity and poor self-control.
7. Review with client on his/her improved status and progress in recovery.

Substance Use Disorder

Adjunct Treatment (Goals and Strategies)

1. AA, NA, or Dual /Diag. group
2. 12- steps group
3. Family therapy
4. Group therapy (Growth Group to deal with dependency issues).
5. Vocational/Rehab counseling
6. Encourage client to join health club, healthy social club, skill training classes and practicing sports to foster a healthy life style.

Schizophrenic Disorder

Immediate Treatment Plan

I. Immediate Concern Treatment Issues
- ◊ Suicide-risk
- ◊ Dangerous to others
- ◊ Psychotic symptoms
- ◊ Substance abuse problem
- ◊ Depression
- ◊ Childhood abuse history
- ◊ Child abuse/Elder abuse
- ◊ Impaired basic self care (homelessness, significant nutritional problem)
- ◊ Other Life Crisis

II. Treatment Plan/Goals
- ◊ To assess the severity of immediate concern issues/crises and to deal with the most severe immediate concern issues and contain them.
- ◊ To assess current stressors and crises and contain them.
- ◊ To proceed with appropriate intervention to address other immediate concern issues and contain them.

III. Intervention Methods
- ◊ Directive/Problem Solving/Supportive Approaches

IV. Strategies

> *** Obtain signed informed consent for treatment (clarify the limits confidentiality in advance and include a clear financial/fee contract.)
> 1. To assess the severity of suicide risk and make necessary intervention.
> 2. Assess danger to others and make necessary interventions. Proceed with mandated report (i.e. Tarasoff) if it is indicated.
> 3. Refer to M.D. for medical evaluation and medication intervention.
> 4. Consider hospitalization if psychotic symptoms are prominent, or the individual's physical condition is gravely impaired.

The Selected Mental Disorders of Adults

> 5. Attend to immediate concern issues of substance abuse and make appropriate intervention.
> 6. Attend to the presented crisis and contain it.
> 7. Attend to other immediate concern issues and make appropriate intervention (i.e. child abuse, elder abuse, homelessness, lack of food resources). Proceed with mandated report if it is indicated.
> 8. If client is a victim of abuse of any type proceed with mandated report if it is indicated and protect from victimization.

Short-Term Treatment Plan

I. Treatment Issues
- ◊ Delusion
- ◊ Hallucination
- ◊ Agitation
- ◊ Cognitive distortion
- ◊ Flat/Blunt Affect
- ◊ Isolation and alienation
- ◊ Sleep problem
- ◊ Poor interpersonal skills
- ◊ Problem with trust (therapeutic alliance issues)
- ◊ Distressed due to mental illness

II. Treatment Plan/Goals
- ◊ To intervene prominent psychotic symptoms.
- ◊ To reduce and eliminate other symptomatic conditions and behaviors.
- ◊ To improve coping skills.
- ◊ To help client to cope with mental illness.

III. Intervention Methods/Approaches
- ◊ Supportive/Cognitive-Behavioral/Psycho-educational Approaches

IV. Strategies

> 1. Establish working and therapeutic alliance with client.
> 2. Do not confront client's lack of interest in therapy
> 3. Do not confront client's delusions and beliefs (confrontation is counter-productive for establishing alliance).

Schizophrenic Disorder

4. Educate client about his/her condition and illness and how the treatment will help symptoms reduction and control the illness.
5. Present client a specific and concrete treatment plan and describe his/her responsibilities in accomplishment of the treatment goals.
6. Do reality testing to deal with delusions.
7. Use stimulus control technique to deal with environmental and interpersonal causes of agitation.
8. Help client to use self monitoring techniques to deal with agitation.
9. Train client to use relaxation technique to deal with agitation and distress.
10. Use cognitive restructuring techniques to deal with cognitive distortions.
11. Train client to use stimulus control, self monitoring, and relaxation techniques to deal with sleep problem.
12. Enroll client in assertiveness training to improve assertiveness and communication skills.
13. Work with client to develop daily structured activity and socialization schedule to deal with isolation and alienation.
14. Use of token economy is appropriate in in-patient and milieu treatment setting.
15. Encourage client to maintain attending psychiatric intervention for psychotic condition.
16. Refer client for comprehensive psychological testing.

Long-Term Treatment Plan

I. Treatment Issues
- ◊ Possible relapse of symptoms
- ◊ Poor self esteem
- ◊ Parental rejection
- ◊ Fear of being mentally ill
- ◊ Internalizing role of patient
- ◊ Poor adaptive social skills
- ◊ Impaired social/interpersonal and vocational functioning
- ◊ Psychotic symptoms

The Selected Mental Disorders of Adults

II. Treatment Plan/ Goals
- ◊ To deal with relapse of symptoms.
- ◊ To deal with underlying issues of low self esteem and parental rejection.
- ◊ To deal with issue of the fear of being mentally ill and internalizing the role of patient.
- ◊ To improve overall life functioning level.

III. Intervention Methods/Approaches
- ◊ Supportive/Psycho-educational Approaches

IV. Strategies

1. Work with client and educate him/her to follow up treatment and therapeutic intervention to prevent relapse of symptoms.
2. Use psycho-educational and supportive approaches to help client in understanding issues related to poor self esteem and parental rejection.
3. Provide safe and therapeutic relationship to help client to deal with and express his/her feelings and fears of being mentally ill.
4. Help client to develop positive feelings about self and others.
5. To help and encourage client in resumption of social/vocational responsibilities to prevent from internalizing role of patient.
6. Work with client to improve overall life functioning level through participation and follow up treatment and participation in Adjunct Treatment.

Adjunct Treatment (Goals and Strategies)

I. Goal:
- ◊ To maintain improved stable condition.

II. Strategies:

1. Family therapy to (1) deal with family members' negative attitudes towards patient in order to decrease negative treatment outcomes (2) encourage their support.

Schizophrenic Disorder

2. Educate family about Schizophrenic Disorders through support group (i.e. Alliance of Mentally Ill).
3. Social Skill Training Group to deal with communication and interpersonal skills problems.
4. Occupational/vocational training
5. Self help and support group for client.
6. Supportive employment program to help client in taking vocational responsibility.

PART III

Application of Treatment Planning and Intervention:
The Personality Disorders of Adults

Part III. Application of Treatment Planning and Intervention: The Personality Disorders of Adults

This section of the book is about treatment of selected personality disorders, with specific approaches of intervention targeting the immediate treatment issues, short-term and symptomatic conditions relevant to a specific personality disorder, and treatment of the long-lasting symptoms and conditions of a specific personality disorder. The first stage of the intervention is to contain crises that may or may not be relevant to the personality disorder. It is to maintain the safety of the patient and to prevent self-harm as well as harm to others. The second stage of the treatment is to intervene for symptoms; conditions, such as mood disturbance, anxiety, impulsivity, fear, transient psychotic symptoms, substance abuse, and sleep disturbance; and therapeutic alliance. A combination of insight-oriented, cognitive-behavioral, and psycho-educational intervention approaches is considered to be effective in dealing with the target symptoms and conditions. This stage of treatment is for symptom reduction, containing troubled conditions, and building up therapeutic alliance.

In treatment of personality disorders, the third stage is the most significant part of the treatment, requiring extended therapy duration and application of insight-oriented therapy and some cognitive-behavioral intervention as the core approach of the treatment. Common treatment issues are fear of rejection, relationship boundaries including therapeutic relationship boundary, dependency needs, poor self-esteem, entitlement, inflated self-esteem, trauma caused by past sexual abuse history, trust issues, poor social or interpersonal skills, and impaired relationship with family or significant others.

Antisocial Personality Disorder

Immediate Treatment Plan

I. Immediate Concern Treatment Issues
- ◊ Suicide-risk (if there is depression)
- ◊ Substance abuse (intoxication)
- ◊ Dangerous to Others
- ◊ Child Abuse
- ◊ Other life crisis (including problems with legal system)

II. Treatment Plan/Goals
- ◊ To assess the severity of immediate concern issues and make appropriate intervention to contain the most severe and potentially dangerous condition.
- ◊ To proceed with appropriate intervention to contain presented crises and other immediate concern issues.

III. Intervention Methods
- ◊ Directive/Problem Solving/Supportive Approaches

IV. Strategies

> *** Obtain a signed informed consent form. Clarify the limits of confidentiality. (Include a clear financial/fee contract).
> 1. To assess the danger to self and make appropriate intervention.
> 2. To assess the danger to others and make appropriate intervention.
> 3. Refer client to hospital or M.D. (If there is drug related intoxication or client indicates sign/symptoms related to medical emergency condition.)
> 4. Attend to crisis issues: (a) assess it; (b) make intervention, and (c) help to contain it.
> 5. Establish therapeutic and working alliance with client (emphasize the positive outcome of the therapeutic intervention; be non-judgmental).

The Personality Disorders of Adults

> 6. If there is any suspicion of child abuse, evidence of elder abuse or dependent abuse, proceed with mandated report and protect victim's safety.

Short-Term Treatment Plan

I. Treatment Issues
- ◊ Resistant to intervention
- ◊ Problem with law and authority
- ◊ Antisocial behavior
- ◊ Drug abuse
- ◊ Job related problems
- ◊ Anger problem
- ◊ Interpersonal/relationship problem
- ◊ Depression

II. Treatment Plan/Goals
- ◊ To encourage client into therapy/deal with resistance to treatment.
- ◊ To reduce symptomatic behavior.
- ◊ To improve coping and interpersonal skills.

III. Intervention Methods
- ◊ Supportive/Directive/Psycho-educational/ Cognitive-Behavioral Approaches

IV. Strategies

> 1. Educate client about the benefits of treatment (saving important relationship or job).
> 2. Confront resistance.
> 3. Use <u>Contingency Management Technique</u> to <u>reinforce</u> positive behavior and cooperation.
> 4. Develop a concrete Treatment Plan indicating target behavior, reinforces and withholding reinforces.
> 5. Provide feedback about improvement and lack of improvement on a planned time frame.
> 6. <u>Role Playing</u> to deal with <u>lack of empathy</u> and <u>lack of sensitivity.</u>
> 7. Train client in using Self Monitoring Technique to deal with antisocial behavior and reduce problems with law and authority.

Antisocial Personality Disorder

> 8. Help client to learn different means of gaining satisfaction and stimulation (less destructive).
> 9. Use self-monitoring to address substance abuse problem (Attending drug/alcohol treatment programs and groups will help with practicing self-monitoring).
> 10. Anger Management Skills Training to deal with anger.
> 11. Relaxation Training to improve constructive coping Skills.

Long-Term Treatment Plan

I. Treatment Issues
- ◊ Belief of Entitlement
- ◊ Poor social sensitivity
- ◊ No sense of respect for social norms and problem with legal system.
- ◊ Impaired family relationship

II. Treatment Plan/ Goals
- ◊ Challenge belief in entitlement.
- ◊ Improve social sensitivity.
- ◊ Deal with family issues.
- ◊ Reduce problem with legal system.

III. Intervention Methods
- ◊ Insight Oriented/Cognitive Approaches

IV. Strategies

> 1. Help client stay in therapy (same as short term therapy).
> 2. Confront psychopathy as a lifestyle (confront client's belief system).
> 3. Challenge beliefs of devaluing others.
> 4. Challenge beliefs of hurting others and not taking responsibility.
> 5. Challenge belief of not receiving consequences for antisocial conduct/behavior.
> 6. Confront client not taking responsibility for his/her negative conduct.
> 7. Deal with family issues, challenge client on importance of his/her behavior in the family (role playing is important).

The Personality Disorders of Adults

Adjunct Treatment (Goals and Strategies):

1. Self Help Group to engender sense of loyalty and responsibility.
2. Self Help group to explore and share feelings.
3. Family Therapy to deal with the pain in the family caused by the client's antisocial conduct.

Avoidant Personality Disorder

Immediate Treatment Plan

I. Treatment Issues
- ◊ Suicide-risk
- ◊ Self medicating/substance abuse
- ◊ Other life crisis
- ◊ Child Abuse
- ◊ Dangerous to Others

II. Treatment Plan/Goals
- ◊ To assess the severity of immediate concern issues and make appropriate intervention to contain the most severe and potentially dangerous condition.
- ◊ To proceed with appropriate intervention to contain presented crises and other immediate concern issues.

III. Intervention Methods
- ◊ Directive/Problem Solving/Supportive Approaches

IV. Strategies

*** Obtain signed informed consent from the patient (clarify the limits confidentiality in advance and include a clear financial/fee contract).
1. To assess the severity of danger to self and make necessary intervention.
2. To assess the danger to others and make appropriate intervention.
3. Refer client for medical evaluation and medication intervention.
4. If any suspicion of child abuse, neglect proceed with mandated report and initiate intervention to protect safety of the child.
5. If he client is a victim of abuse, proceed with the mandated report and protect the victim's safety.
6. Attend to any other immediate concern issues and make appropriate intervention.
7. Attend to the crisis issues and contain the adverse effect of crisis related issues on client.

The Personality Disorders of Adults

Short-Term Treatment Plan

I. Treatment Issues
- Depression/Anxiety
- Trust (therapeutic alliance)
- Isolation
- Poor interpersonal and coping skills
- Fear of intimacy

II. Treatment Plan/Goals
- To reduce symptomatic behavior.
- To improve coping skills.
- To deal with potential for self danger and isolation.
- Foster trust and therapeutic alliance.

III. Intervention Methods
- Supportive/Cognitive-Behavioral/Psycho-educational Approaches

IV. Strategies
1. To develop trust and therapeutic relationship with client
2. Ongoing assessment for potential suicide danger and providing intervention. .
3. Use Cognitive Restructuring technique to reduce depression/anxiety.
4. Relaxation training to deal with anxiety.
5. Avoid confrontation with client on the issue of trust and intimacy confrontation (has adverse effect on therapeutic alliance).
6. Watch for self medicating/substance abuse problem.
7. Provide homework about structured activities between therapy sessions (activities with others).
8. Provide homework or journal writing to note feelings and thoughts.
9. Encourage assertiveness training.
10. Use role playing to improve interpersonal skills.

Avoidant Personality Disorder

Long-Term Treatment Plan

I. Treatment Issues
- ◊ Enduring trust problem
- ◊ Fear of rejection
- ◊ Poor self-esteem
- ◊ Poor social skills

II. Treatment Plan/ Goals
- ◊ Foster trust development.
- ◊ Improve social and interpersonal skills.
- ◊ Promote a positive lifestyle in relating to others.
- ◊ Deal with fear of rejection.

III. Intervention Methods
- ◊ Insight Oriented /Cognitive Approaches

IV. Strategies
1. Assess for depression and potential suicide risk.
2. Deal with underlying issue of trust (interpretation).
3. Deal with underlying issue of fear of rejection and early life trauma (identification, clarification interpretation).
4. Help client to engage and stay in social relationships to deal with ongoing relevant issues related to avoidance.
5. Use covert negative reinforcement (imagining a likely adversative event related to interpersonal relationship, terminate with positive and desired outcome).
6. Deal with underlying issue related to poor self esteem.
7. Confront client if continued avoidance to engage in interpersonal/social relationships with others.

The Personality Disorders of Adults

Adjunct Treatment (Goals and Strategies)

1. Group therapy (Growth group)
2. Family/couples therapy
3. Support, self help group
4. Join some kind of social club (sport, health).
5. Vocational counseling if needed.
6. Social skill training group to deal with interpersonal/social skills.

Borderline Personality Disorder

Immediate Treatment Plan

I. Immediate Concern Treatment Issues
- ◊ Suicide-risk (ideation, thoughts)
- ◊ Substance abuse
- ◊ Childhood abuse history
- ◊ Child abuse
- ◊ Other life crisis (including problems with legal system)

II. Treatment Plan/Goals
- ◊ To assess the severity of suicidal behavior and other immediate concern issues and make appropriate intervention to contain the most severe and potentially dangerous condition.
- ◊ To proceed with appropriate intervention to contain presented crises and other immediate concern issues.

III. Intervention Methods
- ◊ Directive/Problem Solving/Supportive Approaches

IV. Strategies

> *** Obtain signed informed consent from the patient (clarify the limits confidentiality in advance and include a clear financial/fee contract).
> 1. To assess the danger to self and make appropriate intervention.
> 2. Refer client to M.D. for medical evaluation and mediation intervention (if client presents one of following conditions of depression, excessive anxiety, other medical emergency)
> 3. Attend to immediate concern issues related to substance abuse (refer to detoxification).
> 4. If client has child/children, if any suspicion of child abuse, proceed with mandated report and protect child's safety.

The Personality Disorders of Adults

> 5. If any suspicion of child abuse history, proceed with necessary mandated report and protect the safety of the client.
> 6. Attend to any immediate concern issues and make appropriate intervention.
> 7. Attend to the other life crisis and contain it.

Short-Term Treatment Plan

I. Treatment Issues
- ◊ Impulsivity
- ◊ Depression/anxiety
- ◊ Self destructive (transient suicidal ideation)
- ◊ Poor Distress Tolerance
- ◊ Interpersonal relationship problem
- ◊ Substance abuse
- ◊ Anger/acting out on angry impulses
- ◊ Flashback memory of sexual abuse

II. Treatment Plan/Goals
- ◊ To contain ongoing crisis.
- ◊ To reduce/eliminate symptomatic behavior.
- ◊ To improve coping skills.
- ◊ To deal with self- destructiveness.
- ◊ Improve Distress Tolerance.

III. Intervention Methods
- ◊ Supportive/Directive/Psycho-educational/Cognitive-Behavioral/Problem Solving Approaches

IV. Strategies

> 1. Establish working alliance with client (clear boundaries).
> 2. Ongoing assessment for suicidality.
> 3. Set clear limits (time for sessions, phone calls).
> 4. Train client in using Self-Monitoring and Relaxation Skills in dealing with poor distress tolerance.
> 5. Deal with impulsivity (using self-monitoring).
> 6. Use contingency contracting to increase adaptive behavior.

Borderline Personality Disorder

> 7. Use role playing to improve empathy, appropriate expression of emotions, and asking for help.
> 8. Use Cognitive Restructuring to deal with depression and anxiety.
> 9. Use Relaxation Training to deal with anxiety.
> 10. Use anger management skills training to deal with anger (also self monitoring technique, which is appropriate for anger intervention).
> 11. Educate client about less destructive ways to attain gratification.
> 12. Intervene flashback/memories. (Use of systematic desensitization is appropriate).

Long-Term Treatment Plan

I. Treatment Issues:
- Impaired sense of self (not integrated self)
- Interpersonal relationship problems (devaluation of others)
- Problem in handling rejection
- Fear of rejection
- History of sexual abuse

II. Treatment Plan/Goals
- Deal with impaired sense of self.
- Deal with issues related to history of sexual abuse such as pain, shame, and guilt.
- Alter personality structure.
- Promote integration of self.

III. Intervention Methods
- Supportive/Insight Oriented/with some cognitive techniques

IV. Strategies
> 1. Prevent from relapse and crisis.
> 2. Help client to take responsibility and deal with distortion in therapeutic relationship.

The Personality Disorders of Adults

3. Help client to identify and interpret the underlying dynamics of his/her problem behavior.
4. Help client to identify and confront pathological defenses in the interpersonal relationships.
5. Deal with the issue of rejection.
6. Deal and help client in integration of self, deal with impaired sense of self: (a) confront contradictions in behavior, (b) identify split components of self and connections within the self. (Help client to acknowledge splits and connections, and take active participation in therapy process).
7. Help client in process of recovery and re-establish of his/her life.

Adjunct Treatment (Goals and Strategies)

1. Group Therapy
2. Family/Couples Therapy
3. Self Help groups
4. Educational/Vocational Counseling and Training.
5. AA or Daul/Diag groups if there is a drug abuse problem.
6. Sexual abuse support group.

Dependent Personality Disorder

Immediate Treatment Plan

I. Immediate Concern Treatment Issues
- ◊ Suicide-risk
- ◊ Victim of abuse
- ◊ Substance Abuse
- ◊ Other life crisis

II. Treatment Plan/Goals
- ◊ To assess the severity of immediate concern issues and crises.
- ◊ To make appropriate intervention to contain crises and other immediate concern issues.

III. Intervention Methods
- ◊ Directive/Supportive Approaches

IV. Strategies

> *** Obtain signed informed consent from the patient (clarify the limits confidentiality in advance and include a clear financial/fee contract).
> 1. To assess danger to self and make necessary intervention and develop a prevention plan.
> 2. If client is the victim of abuse, proceed to file the mandated report if necessary.
> 3. Refer client to M.D. for medical evaluation and medication intervention.
> 4. Proceed with intervention to deal with immediate concern issues of substance abuse (referral to detoxification).
> 5. Attend to the crisis issues and contain the adverse effect of them on patient (client).

The Personality Disorders of Adults

Short-Term Treatment Plan

    I. Treatment Issues
- Depression
- Poor interpersonal skills (dependency issue)
- Fear of being independent
- Involvement in abusive relationship

    II. Treatment Plan/Goals
- To reduce symptomatic behavior.
- To improve coping and interpersonal skills.
- To deal with abusive relationship pattern.

    III. Intervention Methods
- Supportive/Cognitive-Behavioral Approaches

    IV. Strategies
1. Establish therapeutic alliance with client.
2. Ongoing assessment for suicidality if client is depressed.
3. Use Cognitive Restructuring technique to deal with depression.
4. Use Self Monitoring Technique to decrease engagement in a dependent/abusive relationship.
5. Identify the underlying issues related to abusive relationship (emotional needs, financial needs).
6. Help client to find less destructive ways to deal with his/her needs.
7. Educate client about his/her dependency issues.
8. Foster independent behavior (behavioral rehearsal, role playing homework fostering healthy independent and interdependent behavior).
9. Assertiveness training.
10. Deal with substance dependency/abuse issue, using Self Monitoring Technique.

Long-Term Treatment Plan

    I. Treatment Issues
- Dependency (need for dependency)

Dependent Personality Disorder

- ◊ Fear of rejection
- ◊ Poor self esteem
- ◊ Therapeutic relationship boundaries

II. Treatment Plan/ Goals
- ◊ To reduce dependency needs.
- ◊ Deal with fear of rejection.
- ◊ Foster thoughts and feelings of dependency on him/herself.

III. Intervention Methods
- ◊ Insight Oriented Approach/Cognitive Techniques

IV. Strategies
1. Set clear limits and boundaries with the patient in therapeutic relationship.
2. Deal with underlying issues of abusive relationship.
3. Challenge client with thoughts of the fear of being alone.
4. Challenge constant access to the others.
5. Deal with underlying issue of poor self esteem.
6. Deal with underlying issues and elements related to fear of rejection(identify elements and issues, interpret, and intervene to resolve them).
7. Challenge client with the issue of eliciting intimacy in relationship.
8. Deal with the issue of termination of therapeutic relationship.

Adjunct Treatment

1. Group Therapy
2. Family/Couple Therapy
3. Self Help Group
4. Foster other interests (participating in some skill training classes).

Histrionic Personality Disorder

Immediate Treatment Plan

I. Immediate Concern Treatment Issues
- ◊ Suicide-risk (if depressed and impulsive)
- ◊ Substance abuse
- ◊ Child abuse history (physical/sexual)
- ◊ Medical conditions
- ◊ Other life crisis
- ◊ Child abuse

II. Treatment Plan/Goals
- ◊ To assess the severity of immediate concern issues and make appropriate intervention to contain the most severe and potentially dangerous condition.
- ◊ To proceed with appropriate intervention to contain presented crises and other immediate concern issues.

III. Intervention Methods
- ◊ Directive/Problem Solving/Supportive Approaches

IV. Strategies

> *** Obtain signed informed consent from the patient (clarify the limits confidentiality in advance and include a clear financial/fee contract).
> 1. To assess the danger to self and make appropriate intervention.
> 2. Refer to M.D. for medical evaluation and medication intervention (if depressed, has medical condition).
> 3. Manage immediate issue related to substance abuse (refer to detoxification).
> 4. If client has child/children, if there is any suspicion of child abuse, proceed with mandated report, protect child's safety.
> 5. If client is the victim of abuse, proceed with mandated abuse report, and protect the clients safety.
> 6. Attend to any other immediate concern issues and make appropriate intervention.

The Personality Disorders of Adults

Short-Term Treatment Plan

I. Treatment Issues
- Depression
- Potential self destructive behavior
- Not engaging in therapeutic alliance
- Impulsiveness
- Acting out behavior

II. Treatment Plan/Goals
- To get client to engage in therapeutic process.
- To reduce symptomatic behavior.
- To improve coping skills.
- To deal with potential for self danger.

III. Intervention Methods
- Supportive/Psycho-educational/ Cognitive-Behavioral Approaches

IV. Strategies:
1. Reward engagement in the process of treatment (no financial or incentive rewards)
2. Use reward technique for appropriate accomplishment in therapy.
3. Help client to improve decision making skills using cognitive, restructuring and organization skills.
4. Help client to improve problem solving skills (reward client for attending to the facts and details).
5. Encourage client to attend <u>Assertiveness Training</u> group
6. Relaxation Training to deal with emotional acing out behavior.
7. Use cognitive Restructuring Techniques to deal with depression.
8. Use self monitoring techniques for impulsiveness and acting out.
9. Anger management (if client presents excessive anger), use self monitoring technique and appropriate anger intervention techniques.

Histrionic Personality Disorder

Long-Term Treatment Plan

I. Treatment Issues
- ◊ Dependency
- ◊ Interpersonal relationship problems
- ◊ Avoiding taking responsibility for his/her behavior/decisions.
- ◊ Problem with rejection

II. Treatment Plan/ Goals
- ◊ To enrich client's life by restructuring some of the enduring personality characters, relationship problems and responsibility for behavior/decisions.
- ◊ To deal with <u>dependency</u>, and <u>rejection</u> issues.

III. Intervention Methods
- ◊ Insight Oriented Approach

IV. Strategies
1. Help client to identify and develop insight into his/her dependency needs to others.
2. Deal with early childhood rejection by parents.
3. Help client to understand and have insight into the dynamic of the relationship with the opposite sex (seduction).
4. To deal with transference issue (interpretation, confrontation).
5. To praise patient's real accomplishments in therapy.
6. The therapist should avoid the role of rescuer.
7. Avoid treating client as "special."
8. Interpret defense (denial and flight from therapy).
9. Deal with the demand for affection.

Adjunct Treatment

1. Couples therapy
2. Group therapy (Growth group)
3. Educational/Vocational training
4. Self help group

Schizoid Personality Disorder

Immediate Treatment Plan

I. Immediate Concern Treatment Issues
- ◊ Suicide-risk
- ◊ Dangerous to others
- ◊ Possible active psychotic symptoms
- ◊ History of victimization of others/child abuse
- ◊ Substance abuse
- ◊ Child abuse
- ◊ Basic Self Care difficulty
- ◊ Psychotic symptoms in some cases

II. Treatment Plan/Goals
- ◊ To assess the severity of immediate concern issues and to make appropriate intervention to contain the most severe and potentially dangerous conditions.
- ◊ To proceed with the appropriate intervention to contain presented crisis and other immediate concern issues.

III. Intervention Methods
- ◊ Directive/Problem Solving/Supportive Approaches

IV. Strategies

> *** Obtain signed informed consent for treatment (include a clear financial/fee contract.)
> 1. To assess the potential for suicide and make intervention
> 2. To assess the danger to others and make appropriate intervention. Proceed with "Tarasoff" if it is necessary.
> 3. Refer to M.D. for medical evaluation and medication intervention.
> 4. If client has active psychotic symptoms consider hospitalization.
> 5. If there is any suspicion of child abuse, proceed to do necessary report and make appropriate intervention to protect safety of the child.

The Personality Disorders of Adults

> 6. If client is a victim of abuse of any type, proceed with mandated abuse report and protect the client from victimization.
> 7. Attend to other immediate concern issue of substance abuse (Refer to detoxification).
> 8. Attend to the other immediate concern issues and crises and contain them (basic self care issues).

Short-Term Treatment Plan

I. Treatment Issues
- ◊ Isolation/avoidance
- ◊ Depression/Anxiety
- ◊ Agitation/Anger
- ◊ Psychotic symptoms
- ◊ Psychotic symptoms in some cases
- ◊ Poor interpersonal skills
- ◊ Trust to others problem (therapeutic alliance issues)
- ◊ Possible sleep problem

II. Treatment Plan/Goals
- ◊ To intervene with isolation.
- ◊ To reduce symptomatic behavior (agitation, anger).
- ◊ To improve coping skills.
- ◊ To eliminate/reduce psychotic symptoms.
- ◊ To intervene with depression and sleep problem.

III. Intervention Methods
- ◊ Supportive/Cognitive-Behavioral Approaches

IV. Strategies

> 1. Establish working and therapeutic alliance with client.
> 2. Deal with avoidance, using systematic desensitization, covert modeling.
> 3. Do not confront client's lack of interest and reluctance to be in therapy (it is counterproductive to therapeutic alliance).
> 4. Help client to collect and write down (verbalize) pleasurable memories related to events and interactions with others.

Schizoid Personality Disorder

5. Use cognitive restructuring techniques to deal with depression/anxiety.
6. Relaxation training to deal with anxiety.
7. Assertiveness training to improve communication skills.
8. Role playing to improve interpersonal skills.
9. Train client to use Self Monitoring Techniques to deal with anger/agitation.
10. Homework (structured activity with others).
11. Deal with sleep problem (use Self Monitoring, Stimulus Control Techniques)
12. Encourage client to maintain appointments for psychiatric intervention for psychotic symptoms.
13. Refer client for a comprehensive psychological testing.

Long-Term Treatment Plan

I. Treatment Issues
- ◊ Poor social/interpersonal skills
- ◊ Lack of trust in interpersonal relationship/avoidance
- ◊ Poor self esteem
- ◊ Fear of expression of emotion
- ◊ Impaired vocational functioning
- ◊ Psychotic symptoms in some cases

II. Treatment Plan/ Goals
- ◊ To prevent relapse of symptoms.
- ◊ To deal with underlying issues of fears.
- ◊ To deal with trust issues.
- ◊ To improve overall life functioning skills.

III. Intervention Methods
- ◊ Insight Oriented Approaches/Cognitive-Behavioral Techniques

IV. Strategies

1. Deal with underlying issues of trust in interpersonal relationship (use clarification and interpretation).

The Personality Disorders of Adults

> 2. Deal with underlying issues of poor self esteem. Continue with social skills building.
> 3. Deal with underlying issues of avoidance (identify, interpret).
> 4. To challenge the underlying fears of change and improvement of the emotional regulation routines and expression of emotions.
> 5. Help client to develop positive feelings toward others (identifying the positive elements of client's relationship with others).
> 6. Challenge the idea and issue of the need for space and being a loner.
> 7. Challenge the assumption and idea of being independent and not relating to others.

Adjunct Treatment (Goals and Strategies)

> 1. Group Therapy (Supportive Approach).
> 2. Self Help group (For sharing feelings).
> 3. To involve him/herself in some kind of social club (socialization, sports, activities).
> 4. Vocational counseling if needed.
> 5. Vocational training and supportive employment.

References

Aguitera, Donna E. (1994). *Crisis intervention: theory and methodology*. St. Louis, Mo.: The C.V. Mosby Company.

Akhtar, S. (1986). Differentiating schizoid and avoidant personality disorders. *American Journal of Psychiatry*, 143: 1061 – 1062.

Anastopolous, A., Shelton, T., DuPaul, G., Guevremont, D. (1993). Parent training for attention-deficit hyperactivity disorder: its impact on parent functioning. *Journal of Abnormal Child Psychology.* 21, 581 – 596.

Beardslee, W. R., Bemporad, J., Keller, M.B., & Klerman, G.L. (1973). Children of parents with major affective disorder: a review. *American Journal of Psychiatry*, 140, 825 – 32.

Beck, A. T., Rush, A. J., Shaw, B. E. & Emery, G. (1979). *Cognitive theory of depression.* New York; Guilford Press.

Benjamin, Lorna Smith. (1996). *Interpersonal diagnosis and treatment of personality disorders*. New York: Guilford Press.

Bernstein, D. P., Useda, D., Slever, L. (1993). Paranoid personality disorder. review of the literature of recommendations for DSM-IV. *Journal of Personality Disorders*, 7, 53 -62.

Biederman, J. A., Munir, K., & Knee, D. (1987). Conduct and oppositional disorder in clinically referred children with attention deficit disorder: a controlled family study. *Journal of the American Academy of Child and Adolescent Psychiatry*, 26, 724 – 27.

Brenner, J. Douglas. (1998). *Trauma, memory, and dissociation.* Washington, DC: American Psychiatric Press.

References

Cantwell, D. (1994). *Therapeutic management of attention deficit disorder: participant workbook.* New York: SCP Communication.

Carson, R.C., & Butcher, J. N. (1992). *Abnormal psychology and modern life.* (9th Ed.). New York: Harper Collins.

Cocciarella, A., Wood, R. & Low, K. (1995). Brief behavioral treatment for attention-deficit hyperactivity disorder. *Perceptual & Motor Skills*, 8, 225 – 226.

Cohen, P., Cohen, J., & Brook, J. (1993a). An epidemiological study of disorders in late childhood and adolescence – II persistence of disorders. *Journal of Child Psychology and Psychiatry*, 34, 869 – 77.

Cohen, Sidney (Editor), (1986). *The diagnosis & treatment of drug and alcohol abuse.* New York: Haworth Press.

Combs, A. W. (1989). *A theory of therapy: guidelines for the counseling practice.* Newbury Park, Ca: Sage.

Cotler, I. B., Compton, W. M. III, Mager, D., Spitznagel, E. L. & Janea, A. (1992). Post-traumatic stress disorder and substance abusers for the general population. *American Journal of Psychiatry*, 149, 664 – 670.

Counts, R. M. (1990). The concept of dissociation. *Journal of the American Academy of Psychoanalysis.* 18(3): 460 – 479.

Davidson, J. R. T. & Foa, E. B., (1991). Diagnostic issues in post-traumatic stress disorder: considerations for the DSM – IV. *Journal of Abnormal Psychology*, 100, 346 – 353.

Davidson, Richard J. (1998). *Neuropsychological perspecties on affective & anxiety disorders.* East Sussex, UK: Psychology Press.

References

Eckberg, M. (2000). *Victims of cruelty. somatic psychotherapy in the healing of posttraumatic stress disorder*. Berkeley, CA. North Atlantic Book.

Everett, Craig A. (1999).*Family therapy for ADHD: treating children, adolescents and adults*. New York: Guilford Press.

Fairbank, J. A. & Keane, T. M. (1982). Flooding for combat-related stress disorders: assessment of anxiety reduction across traumatic memories. *Behavior Therapy*, 13.499 – 510.

Fisher, Sheila A. (1973). *Suicide & crisis intervention: survey and guide to services*. New York, NY: Springer Publishing Co.

Foa, E. B., Olasov-Rothbaum, B., Riggs, D. S. & Murdock, T. B. (1991). Treatment of post-traumatic stress disorder in rape victims: a comparison between cognitive-behavioral procedures and counseling. *Journal of Counseling and Clinical Psychology*, 59, 715 – 723.

Garber, J., Kriss, M. R., Koch, M. & Lindholm, L. (1988). Recurrent depression n adolescents: a follow-up study. *Journal of the American Academy of Child Psychiatry*, 27, 49 – 54.

Golan, Naomi. (1978). Treatment in crisis situations. New York: The Free Press.

Goldberg, Richard J., Slaby, Andrew E. (1981). *Diagnosing disorders of the mood, thought and behavior*. Garden City, N.Y.: Medical Examination Pub. Co.

Goodyer, Ian M. (1995). *The depressed child & adolescents: developmental and clinical perspectives*. Cambridge, Eng.: Cambridge University Press.

Greenberg, R. P. & Bornstein, R. F., (1988). The dependent personality:1- risk for physical disorders, *Journal of Personality Disorders,* 2, 126 – 135.

Grigoroiu-Seranescu, M., Christodoesu, D., Magureanu, S., et al, (1991). Adolescent offpring of endogenous unipolar depressive parents and of normal parents. *Journal of Affective Disorders*, 21, 185 – 198.

References

Gunderson, J. G. Zanarini, M. C., & Kisiel, C. L. (1991). Borderline personality disorder: a review of data on DSM-III-R descriptions, *Journal of Personality Disorders,* 5, 340 – 352.

Hammon, C. (1991). *Depression runs in families: the social context of risk and resilience in children of depressed parents.* New York, NY: Springer-Verlag.

Harrington, Richard. (1993). *Depressive disorder in childhood & adolescents.* Chichester, NY: Wiley.

Harrington, R. C., Fidge, H., Rutter, M., et al, (1990). Adult outcomes of childhood and adolescent depression: I. psychiatric status. *Archives of General Psychiatry,* 47, 465 – 73.

Harris, C. J., (1991). A family crisis-intervention model for the treatment of post traumatic stress reaction. *Journal of Traumatic Stress,* 4, 195 – 207.

Jensen, J., Burke, N., & Garfinkel, B. (1988). Depression & symptoms of attention deficit disorder with hyperactivity. *Journal of American Academy of Child and Adolescent Psychiatry,* 27, 742 – 747.

Johnson, D. (1987). The role of creative arts therapies in the diagnosis and treatment of psychological trauma. *Arts in Psychotherapy,* 14, 7 – 14.

Josephson, Martin M. (1979). *Clinician's handbook of childhood psychopathology.* New York, NY: Jason Aronson.

Keane, T. M., Gerardi, R. J., Quinn, S. J., Littz, B. T. (1992). Behavioral treatment of post-traumatic stress disorder. In S. M.Turner, K. S. Calhoun & H. E. Adams (eds). *Handbook of clinical behavior therapy* (2nd Ed). New York: Wiley.

Kovacs, M. & Goldston, D. (1991). Cognitive and social cognitive development of depressed children and adolescents. *Journal of the American Academy of Child Psychiatry,* 20, 388 -92.

References

Kovacs, M. & Paulauskas, S. L. (1984). Developmental state and the expression of depressive disorders in children: an empirical analysis. In D. Cicchetti & K. Schneider-Rosen (eds), *Childhood depression (New direction for child development, no. 26)*. San Francisco, Ca: Josscy-Barr, pp. 59 -80.

Kupersmidt, J. B. & Patterson, C. J., (1991). Childhood peer rejection, aggression, withdrawal, and perceived competence as apredictors of self-reported behavior problems in preadolescence. *Journal of Abnormal Child Psychology*, 19, 427 – 449.

Kupfer, D. (1992). Maintenance treatment on recurrent depression: current and future directions. *British Journal of Psychiatry*, 161, 309 – 16.

Kutcher, S. & Marton, P. (1991). Affective disorders in first degree relatives of adolescent onset bipolar, unipolars, and normal controls. *Journal of the American Academy of Child Psychiatry*, 30, 75-78.

Langlsley, Donald G. (1968). *The treatment of families in crisis*. New York, NY: Grune & Stratton.

Larsson, B. & Melin, L. (1990). Depressive symptoms in Swedish adolescents. *Journal of Abnormal Child Psychology*, 18, 91 – 103.

Larsson, B., Melin, L., Breitholtz, E. & Anderson, G. (1991). Short-term stability of depressive symptoms and suicide attempts in Swedish adolescents. *Acta Psychiatrica Scandinavia*, 83, 385 – 90.

Leff, M. J., Roatch, J. F. & Bunney, W. E. (1970). Environmental factors preceding the onset of severe depressions. *Psychiatry*, 33, 293 – 311.

Lester, David & Brockopp, Gene W. (1973). *Crisis intervention & counseling by telephone*. Springfield, Il.: Charles C. Thomas.

References

Levine, Peter A. (2010). *In an unspoken voice: how the body releases trauma and restores goodness*. Berkeley, CA. North Atlantic Book.

Linehan, M. M. (1993). *Cognitive-behavioral therapy and border-line personality disorder*. New York, NY: Guildford Press.

Livingston, R., Nugent, H., Rader, L. & Smith, G. R. (1983). Family histories of depressed and severely anxious children. *American Journal of Psychiatry*, 142, 1497 – 1499.

Marthunen, M. J., Aro, H. M., Henrikron, M. M., Lonnqvist, J. K. (1991). Mental disorders in adolescent suicide, DSM-III-R axes I and axes II- diagnosis in suicides 13 – 19 year olds in Finland. *Archives of General Psychiatry*, 48, 834 – 839.

Matson, J. L. (1987). *Treating depression in children and adolescents*. New York, NY: Pergamum.

McCauley, E., Carlson, G.A. & Calderon, R. (1991). The role of somatic complaints in the diagnosis of depression in children and adolescents. *Journal of the American Academy of Child Psychiatry*, 30, 631 – 3.

McClellan, J. M., Rubert, M. P., Reichler, R. J. & Sylvester, C. E. (1990). Attention deficit disorder in children at risk for anxiety and depression. *Journal of the American Academy of Child Psychiatry*, 29, 534 – 539.

McFarlane, A. (1992). Avoidance and intrusion in post-traumatic disorder. *Journal of Nervous and Mental Disease*, 180(7), 439 – 445.

Meadows, E. A. & Foa, E. B. (1999). Cognitive-behavioral treatment of traumatized adults. In P. A. Saigh & J. D. Bremner (Eds) *Posttraumatic stress disorder: a comprehensive textbook*. Needham Heights, Ma: Allyn & Bacon.

Mendelwicz, J. & Baron, M. (1981). Morbidity risks in subtypes of unipolar depressive illness: differences between early and late onset forms. *British Journal of Psychiatry*, 139, 463 – 466.

References

Meyer, Robert G. (1989). *The clinician's handbook: the psychopathology of adulthood & adolescence.* Boston, Ma: Allyn & Bacon.

Meyer, Robert G. (1996). *The clinician's handbook: integrated diagnostic, assessment and intervention in adult and adolescent psychopathology.* Boston, Ma: Allyn & Bacon.

Miller, W. R. & DePilato, M. (1983). Treatment of nightmares via relaxation and desensitization: a controlled evaluation. *Journal of Counseling and Clinical Psychology*, 51, 870 – 877.

Munoz, Rodrigo A. (Editor) (1984). *Therapeutic potential of mood disorder clinics.* San Francisco, Ca.: Jossey-Bass.

Nelson, J. C. & Charney, D. S. (1981). The symptoms of major depressive illness. *American Journal of Psychiatry*, 138, 1 – 13.

Nolen-Hoeksema, S., Girgus, J. S. & Saligman, M. E. P. (1992). Predictors and consequences of childhood depressive symptoms: a 5-year longitudinal study. *Journal of Abnormal Psychology*, 101, 405 – 422.

Oates, R. K., Forrest, D. & Peacock, A. (1985). Self-esteem of abused children. *Child Abuse and Neglect*, 9, 159 – 163.

Oster, G. D. & Cara, J. E. (1990). *Understanding and treating depressed adolescents and their families.* New York, NY: John Wiley.

Paykel, E. S. (1989). Treatment of depression: the relevance of research for clinical practice. *British Journal of Psychiatry*, 155, 754 – 763.

Penk, W. E., Keane, T. M., Rabinowitz, R., Fowler, D. R., Bell, W. E. & Finkelstien, A. (1988). Post-traumatic stress disorder. In R. Greene (Ed.). *The MMPI: use with specific populations.* New York, NY: Gruen & Stratton, 193 – 213.

References

Peterson, C., Prout, M. & Schwarz, R. (1991). *Post-traumatic stress disorder: a clinician's guidebook.* New York, NY: Plenum Press.

Pfeffer, C. R. (1992). Relationship between depression and suicidal behavior. In *Clinical guide to depression in children and adolescents* Ed. M Schafii & S. L. Shafii, pp. 115 – 126. Washington, D.C.: American Psychiatric Press.

Pfeffer, C., Klerman, G. L., Hunt, S. W., Lesser, M., Peskin, J. R. & Siefker, C. A. (1991).Suicidal children grown up: demographic and clinical risk factors for adolescent suicidal attempts. *Journal of the American Society of Child Psychiatry*, 30, 609 – 616.

Prior, M. (1992). Childhood tempermemt. *Journal of Child Psychology and Psychiatry*, 33, 249 – 279.

Puig-Antich, J., Lukens, E., Davies, M. Gortz, D., Brennan-Quiltrock, J. & Todak, G. (1985b). Psychosocial functioning in prepubertal major depressive disorders, II: interpersonal relationships after sustained recovery from affective episode. *Archives of General Psychiatry*, 42, 511 – 517.

Quinton, D. & Rutter, M. (1985). Family pathology and child psychiatric disorder: a four year prospective study. In A.R. Nicol (Ed). *Longitudinal Studies in Child Psychology and Psychiatry.* Chichester, NY: John Wiley.

Radke-Yarrow, M. & Sherman, T. (1990). Hard growing children who survive. In J. Rolf, A. Mastan, D. Ciccheti, Nuechterlein & S. Weintraub (Eds), *Relationships within families: mutual influences.* Cambridge, Eng.: Cambridge University Press.

Radloff, L. S. (1977). A CES-D scale: a self report depression scale for research in the general population. *Applied Psychology Measurement*, 1, 385 – 401.

Range, P. A. & Schnicke, M. K. (1990). Long-term bereavement from suicide, homicide, accidents and natural deaths. *Death Studies,* 14, 423 – 433.

References

Reich, W. & Earle, T. (1987)/ Rules for making psychiatric diagnosis in children on the basis of multiple sources of information: preliminary strategies. *Journal of Abnormal Child Psychology*, 15, 601 – 616.

Rehm, L. P. (1977). A self-control model of depression. *Behavior Therapy*, 8, 787 – 804.

Resnick, P. A. & Schnicke, M. K. (1993). *Cognitive processing therapy for rape victims: a treatment manual*. Newbury Park, Ca: Sage.

Reynolds, W. M. & Coats, K. I. (1986). A cmparson of cognitive-behavioral therapy and relaxation training for the treatment of depression in adolescents. *Journal of Consulting & Clinical Psychology*, 54, 653 – 660.

Reynolds, W. M. (1990). Development of a semistructural clinical interview for suicidal behavior in adolescents. *Psychological Assessment: A Journal of Consulting and Clinical Psychology*, 2, 382 – 290.

Reynolds, William Michael (1994). *Handbook of depression in children & adolescents*. New York, NY: Plenum Press.

Rozynkov,V. & Dondershine, H. (1991). Trauma focus group therapy for Vietnam veterans with DTSD. *Psycholtherapy*, 28(1), 157 – 161.

Saigh, Philip, A. (1999). *Posttraumatic stress disorder: a comprehensive text*. Boston, Ma: Allyn & Bacon.

Saigh, P. A. (1992a). The behavioral trarment of child and adolescent posttraumatic stress disorder. *Advances in Behavior Research and Treaty*, 14, 247 – 275.

Schore, J. & Schore, A. (2008). Modern attachment theory: the central role of affect regulation in development and treatment. *Clinical Social work Journal*, 36 (1), 9-20.

References

Seligman, M. E. P. & Peterson, C. (1986). A learned helpless perspective on childhood depression: theory and research. In *Depression in young people: developmental and clinical perspectives*. M. Rutter, C. E. Izard & P. B. Read (Eds), pp. 223 -50. New York, NY: Guilford Press.

Shearer, S. L., Peters, C. P., Quaytman, M. S. & Ogden, R. L. (1990). Frequency and correlates of childhood sexual and physical abuse histories in adult female borderline inpatients. *American Journal of Psychiatry*, 15, 214 – 216.

Simon, Alexander, Lowenthal, M. F. & Epstein, L. J. (1970). *Crisis and intervention: the fate of the elderly mental patient*. San Francisco, Ca.: Jossey-Bass, Inc. Publishers.

Sperry, Len (1995). *Handbook of diagnosis and treatment of the DSM-IV personality disorder*. New Your, NY: Brunner/Mazel.

Stein, D. J. Hollander, E. & Skodel, A. E. (1993). Anxiety disorders & personality disorders: a review. *Journal of Personality Disorders*, 7, 87 – 104.

Warner, V., Weirman, M. M., Fendrich, M., et al, (1992). The causes of major depression in the offspring of depressed parents: incidence, recurrence, and recovery. *Archives of General Psychiatry*, 49, 795 – 801.

Wender, E. (1995). Attention-deficit hyperactivity disorders in adolescences. *Journal of Development & Behavioral Pediatrics*, 16, 192 – 195.

Werry, J. S., McClellan, J. M. & Chard, L. (1991). Childhood & adolescent schizophrenic, bipolar, and schizoaffective disorders: a clinical and outcome study. *Journal of the American Academy of Child Psychiatry*, 30, 457 – 65.

Whybrow, Peter C. (1987). *A mood apart: depression, mania, and other afflictions of the self*. New York, NY: Basic Books.

Williams, Linda Myer (1999). *Trauma & Memory*. Thousand Oaks, Ca.: Sage Publications.

References

Williams, Mary Beth & Sommer, John F. (1994). *Handbook of post-traumatic therapy.* Westport, Ct.: Greenwood, Press.

Wilson, J. P. & Lindy, J. (1994). *Countertransference in the treatment of post-traumatic stress disorders.* New York, NY: Guilford Press.

Wolpe. J. (1990). The practice of behavioral therapy (4th Ed). Elmsford, NY: Pergamon.

Yalom, Irvin D. (1985). *The theory and practice of group psychotherapy.* (3rd Ed). New York, NY: Basic Books.

Zeitlin, H. (1986). The natural history of psychiatric disorder in children. Oxford, Eng.: Oxford University Press.

Zubin, Joseph, Freyham, Fritz A. (1972). *Disorders of mood.* Baltimore, Md.: The Johns Hopkins University Press.

CPSIA information can be obtained at www.ICGtesting.com
Printed in the USA
BVOW08s1149031214

377597BV00005B/20/P